Starting
with
Prefixes and
Suffixes

defrost

tricycle

prehistoric

Authors

Timothy Rasinski, Ph.D.

Nancy Padak, Ed.D.

Rick M. Newton, Ph.D.

Evangeline Newton, Ph.D.

SHELL EDUCATION

Consultant

Tiffany Fadin, M.A.Ed.
Teacher and Reading Specialist

Publishing Credits

Dona Herweck Rice, *Editor-in-Chief*; Robin Erickson, *Production Director;*
Lee Aucoin, *Creative Director;* Timothy J. Bradley, *Illustration Manager;*
Sara Johnson, M.S.Ed., *Editorial Director*; Evelyn Garcia, *Associate Education Editor;*
Leah Quillian, *Assistant Editor;* Grace Alba, *Designer;*
Corinne Burton, M.A.Ed., *Publisher*

Image Credits
p.52, 76, 83, 84, 97, 106, Dreamstime; p.76, 157, 158, Bigstock; p.78, 88, 130 iStockphoto; all other images Shutterstock

Standard
© 2004 Mid-continent Research for Education and Learning (McREL)
© 2010 National Governors Association Center for Best Practices and Council of Chief State School Officers (CCSS)

Shell Education

5301 Oceanus Drive
Huntington Beach, CA 92649-1030
http://www.shelleducation.com
ISBN 978-1-4258-1103-7
© 2013 Shell Educational Publishing, Inc.
Printed in USA. WOR004

Table of Contents

Why Roots?
Vocabulary Research and Practice

What Is a Root?

A root is a word part that contains meaning (and not merely sound). There are three categories of roots, depending on their placement in a word:

- prefix: a root at the beginning of a word. For example, in the word *retraction*, the initial *re-* is a prefix, meaning "back, again."

- base: the core root, which provides a word with its basic meaning. In the word *retraction*, the base is *tract*, which means "pull, draw, drag."

- suffix: a root that ends a word. In the word *retraction*, the final *-ion* is a suffix, meaning "act of, state of."

What Do Prefixes and Suffixes Do?

A prefix serves one of three functions:

- A prefix can *negate* a word by meaning "not." The most common negating prefixes are *un-* (e.g., unhappy, unwashed) and negative *in-, im-, il-* (e.g., invisible, impossible, illegal). Some directional prefixes can also be negating. For example, the prefix variations *di-, dis-, dif-*, which mean "apart, in different directions," can also mean "not." Examples: things that are "not similar" are *dissimilar*; a *difficult* task is "not" easy.

- A prefix can be *directional.* This is the most common function of a prefix: it sends the base of the word in a specific direction. The prefix *ex-* means "out," *re-* means "back, again," *sub-* means "under, below," and *ad-* means "to, toward, add to." For example, an *exit* sign indicates the way "out" of a building; we *descend* a staircase when we go "down"; when class *convenes*, it comes "together"; when class is *dismissed*, students scatter "in different directions";

when they *proceed* to their buses, they move "forward, ahead" to their bus stops.

Thus, using the base *tract-* (pull, draw, drag), *extract* means to "pull out" (e.g., we extract a tooth); *retract* means to "take or pull back" (e.g., a journalist retracts a statement; a cat retracts its claws); *subtract* means to "take a lower number from a higher one"; to *attract* means to "pull, draw someone to or toward an object" (the prefix *at-* in this word is assimilated *ad-*; e.g., a magnet attracts metal objects, which are "pulled toward" it).

- A prefix can have *intensifying force,* meaning "very, thoroughly." A *perfectly* baked cake, for example, is "thoroughly" done.

A suffix either changes the part of speech (e.g., *act, action*) or modifies the base (e.g., *fast, faster*).

> **Note:** Although students may not be aware that prefixes can suggest direction, they can benefit from examining the prefix and thinking about the direction of these words (both literal and metaphorical).

Why Roots?
Vocabulary Research and Practice (cont.)

What Is Assimilation?

Some prefixes have multiple forms, as shown in the chart on page 8. These slight changes reflect an easily recognizable and predictable phenomenon called *assimilation*. Assimilation simply means that some consonants at the beginning of a word change and become like the consonants that follow them (*assimilate* = "similar to").

It is obvious that the prefix *con-*, for example, occurs in the words *convention* and *conference*. Through assimilation, a variation of *con-* also appears in *collect, commotion,* and *correct.* The reason is simple: assimilation makes a word easier to pronounce (consider *conlect* vs. *collect*).

The concept of assimilation can be easily understood and presented in a three-step approach. The three steps are: (1) unassimilated prefixes (i.e., the prefix is not changed since it is easily pronounced with the next letter of the word), as in *convention, invent, advent, subterranean;* (2) partial assimilation (i.e., the prefix changes its final *n-* into an *m-* to facilitate pronunciation with the next letter of the word), as in *compose, imbibe, import;* and (3) full assimilation (i.e., the prefix changes its final consonant into the same consonant as the next letter of the word to facilitate pronunciation), which results in a doubled consonant, as in *collect, illegal, attract, suffer, support.*

Unassimilated prefixes thus retain their original form as *con-, in-, ad-, sub-,* and so on. Partial assimilation occurs when prefixes that end in *n-* (e.g., *con-, in-*) change to *m-* before bases that begin with *b-* or *p-*: *con + bine* becomes *combine*, for example. Full assimilation occurs when the final consonant of the prefix is dropped and the following consonant doubled: *con + lect* becomes *collect*, and *ad + tract* becomes *attract*.

Although assimilation causes spelling changes, the meaning of the prefix does not change. The Teaching Tips section will let you know if the prefix for a particular lesson can undergo assimilation. Suffixes, however, do not undergo assimilation.

To teach assimilation, explain the concept to students by showing them a few examples, such as the ones provided in the chart (page 8). As you discuss these examples, be sure that students recognize the prefix of the word. Tell them that whenever a doubled consonant appears near the beginning of a word, they should divide the word between the doubled consonant and identify the assimilated prefix. Also, remind them that *con-* and *in-* may partially assimilate and become *com-* or *im-* when they attach to bases that begin with *b-* or *p-*.

See the following page for an outline of the three-step approach to presenting assimilation. This approach uses examples of commonly known words, which can be helpful when introducing the concept. In each step, ask students to pronounce the prefix and base separately. Then, ask them to pronounce the prefix and the base together as a single word. In Step 1, pronunciation is easy without altering the prefix. In Step 2, partial assimilation makes the prefix easier to pronounce with the base. In Step 3, full assimilation is required to make the prefix easier to pronounce, resulting in a double consonant near the beginning of the word.

Why Roots?
Vocabulary Research and Practice *(cont.)*

Step 1: Unassimilated Prefixes

con + vention = convention

in + visible = invisible

sub + terranean = subterranean

ob + struction = obstruction

ex + pose = expose

dis + tract = distract

> **Note:** We can easily pronounce the unaltered prefix with the base. Hence, there is no need to assimilate.

Step 2: Partial Assimilation

in + possible = impossible

con + pose = compose

con + bine = combine

con + fort = comfort

> **Note:** We cannot easily pronounce *n* when it is followed by such consonants as *b, p,* and (occasionally) *f.* In such cases, the final *n* of the prefix partially assimilates into *m.*

Step 3: Full Assimilation

con + rect = correct

in + legal = illegal

sub + fer = suffer

ob + pose = oppose

ex + fect = effect

dis + fer = differ

ad + similation = assimilation

> **Note:** We cannot easily pronounce these unaltered prefixes when followed by certain consonants. In such cases, the final consonant of the prefix changes into the initial consonant of the base that follows it. The result is a doubled consonant near the beginning.

Why Roots?
Vocabulary Research and Practice *(cont.)*

Latin Prefixes that Assimilate

Prefix	Meaning	Examples
ad-	to, toward, add to	*admit, accelerate, affect, aggravate, allusion, appendix, arrogant, assimilate, attract*
con-, co-	with, together, very	*congregate, coworker, collect, combine, commit, compose, correct*
ex-, e-, ef-	out, from, completely	*expose, edict, effect*
dis-, di-, dif-	apart, in different directions, not	*disintegrate, divert, different, difficult*
in-, im-, il- (directional)	in, on, into, against	*induct, insert, imbibe, immigrant, import, impose, illustrate*
in-, im-, il- (negative)	not	*infinite, insatiable, ignoble, illegal, illegible, impossible, irresponsible*
ob-	toward, up against	*obstruct, occurrence, offensive, oppose*
sub-	under, up from under	*submarine, succeed, suffer, support, suspend*

Why Teach with a Roots Approach?

Teaching with a roots approach is efficient. Over 60 percent of the words students encounter in their reading have recognizable word parts (Nagy et al. 1989). Moreover, content-area vocabulary is largely of Greek and Latin origin (Harmon, Hedrick, and Wood 2005). Many words from Greek and Latin roots meet the criteria for "tier two" words and are appropriate for instruction (Beck, McKeown, and Kucan 2002).

Root study also promotes independent word learning (Carlisle 2010). In addition, students learn to make connections among words that are semantically related (Nagy and Scott 2000). Research suggests that the brain is a pattern detector (Cunningham 2004). Latin and Greek word roots follow linguistic patterns that can help students with the meaning, sound, and spelling of English words. Indeed, Latin and Greek roots have consistent orthographic (spelling) patterns (Rasinski and Padak 2008; Bear et al. 2011).

Young readers' word instruction is often characterized by a study of word patterns called rimes. A Latin-Greek roots approach is the next logical and developmental step in word learning (Bear et al. 2011). Many English language learners speak first languages semantically related to Latin (e.g., Spanish, which is a "Romance" [Latin-derived] language). Enhancing this natural linguistic connection can accelerate these students' vocabulary growth (Blachowicz et al. 2006).

Many states are beginning to include a study of derivations in their elementary and middle school literacy standards. Indeed, the new Common Core State Standards (National Governors Association Center for Best Practices and Council of Chief State School Officers 2011) focus extensively on root-specific standards in the "Reading: Foundational Skills" and "Language" sections. According to these standards, attention to roots should begin in kindergarten. (For more information, see http://www.corestandards.org/.)

What Does Research Say About Using a Roots Approach?

The size and depth of elementary students' vocabulary is associated with proficiency in reading comprehension. Effective vocabulary instruction results in higher levels of reading comprehension (Baumann et al. 2002; Beck et al. 1982; Kame'enui, Carnine, and Freschi 1982; Stahl and Fairbanks 1986).

Morphological analysis (e.g., a roots approach) is important because it is generative and allows students to make connections among semantically related words or word families (Nagy and Scott 2000). In fact, developing morphological awareness is an integral component of word learning for young children (Biemiller and Slonim 2001). In a comprehensive review of 16 studies analyzing the effect of instruction in morphological awareness on literacy achievement, Carlisle (2010) observes that "children learn morphemes as they learn language" (465).

Classroom-based studies have demonstrated the effectiveness of teaching word parts and context clues (Baumann et al. 2005) in the primary (Biemiller 2005; Mountain 2005; Porter-Collier 2010) and intermediate grades (Baumann et al. 2002; Carlisle 2000; Kieffer and Lesaux 2007). Research in content-area vocabulary has demonstrated the effectiveness of teaching Greek and Latin word roots, especially for struggling readers (Harmon, Hedrick, and Wood 2005).

No single instructional method is sufficient. Teachers need a variety of methods that teach word meanings while also increasing the depth of word knowledge (Blachowicz et al. 2006; Lehr, Osborn, and Hiebert 2011). These methods should aim at the following:

- **Immersion.** Students need frequent opportunities to use new words in diverse oral and print contexts in order to learn them thoroughly (Blachowicz and Fisher 2009).

- **Metacognitive and metalinguistic awareness.** Students must understand and know how to manipulate the structural features of language (Nagy and Scott 2000).

- **Word consciousness** (e.g., an awareness of and interest in words) (Graves and Watts-Taffe 2002). Word exploration (e.g., etymology) and word play (e.g., puns, riddles) are central to vocabulary development (Lehr, Osborn, and Hiebert 2011).

Differentiating Instruction

To make *Starting with Prefixes and Suffixes* most effective, you may want to differentiate instruction for students who have particular needs. Groups of students who may benefit from differentiated instruction include English language learners, struggling readers, above-level readers, and students with special needs. The sections that follow offer some instructional suggestions for each group of students.

Supporting English Language Learners

Like their peers, English language learners benefit from the focus on meaning using research-based strategies to learn new roots and words. Frequent opportunities to try new words out in a variety of contexts will help English language learners, as will partner or small-group work, which has the additional advantage of supporting English language learners' conversational English. Especially if students' native languages derive from Latin (e.g., Spanish), make comparisons to the native languages whenever possible. (You can look online for resources to assist with this. The website http://spanish.about.com/od /spanishvocabulary/a/spanishprefixes.htm compares Spanish and English prefixes. Additionally, the chart found at http://www .colorincolorado.org/pdfs/articles/cognates .pdf compares Spanish and English bases.) When they learn to look for roots within words, Spanish speakers will be able to relate many word roots in English to their counterparts in Spanish. Sharing their knowledge with other classmates will help everyone grow.

You may need to provide additional time for English language learners to complete activities. You may also need to add context to activities, to make certain that new words appear in the context of sentences. For example, you (or a tutor or peer) can read sentences aloud to these students, then ask them to read the sentences with you, and finally invite independent responses.

Concrete context will also support English language learners' work with prefixes, suffixes, and words. You can use gestures or body language to provide nonlinguistic support when possible. You can also provide (or ask students to make) word cards for them to manipulate or word banks with answers to select from. Flashcards of the prefixes and suffixes in this book are provided in Appendix C and in the Digital Resources (prefixesflashcards.pdf, suffixesflashcards.pdf, blankflashcards.pdf).

Supporting Struggling Readers

Struggling readers will benefit from extra support and instructional time. You may want to do a few examples with them before encouraging independent response. Making activities more concrete and providing word banks for answers will also help. Students might work with partners to complete activities. You will want to monitor struggling readers' progress and make adjustments as needed.

Supporting Above-Level Readers

Above-level readers may not need all the examples provided in the lessons to understand the concepts being taught. You may want to have students complete only the most challenging examples. Often, above-level readers will enjoy additional challenges. You may want them to develop their own activities using prefixes or suffixes for others to complete. The Internet offers tools for making crossword puzzles and other word games that students may develop themselves to challenge their peers (e.g., http://www.puzzlemaker.com).

Above-level students may be interested in peer tutoring as well. They may also lead efforts to find words using the prefixes or suffixes of focus in other texts. However, it is important to ensure that the extra challenges you provide are more fun than busywork.

Differentiating Instruction *(cont.)*

Supporting Students with Special Needs

Response to Intervention (RTI) is an approach to instructional delivery for students who struggle with or have special needs in some aspect of learning (Griffiths et al. 2007). The RTI model has three levels of intensity. The first level, or tier, is for the majority of students (about 75–80 percent) who benefit from universal instruction. The second tier is for a smaller percentage of students (10–15 percent) in a classroom; these students need more targeted instruction because universal instruction does not enable them to be successful. This instruction typically involves adaptations that a general education teacher can reasonably accomplish (Fuchs and Fuchs 1998), such as providing extra time, additional lessons, extra instructional materials such as concrete visual scaffolds, or other adjustments in support. The third tier includes the smallest percentage of students (5–10 percent): those who do not respond sufficiently to Tier II instruction and who likely need to be screened for special education placement.

The following are some ideas for using the RTI model to differentiate instruction with *Starting with Prefixes and Suffixes*:

- **Tier I:** Encourage peer work. Students who are above level may need additional challenges.

- **Tier II:** Arrange peer work. If possible, provide instruction in small groups and increase instructional time. Monitor progress more frequently than with Tier I students. Provide additional practice. Involve parents. Encourage use of graphics (e.g., word webs) and pictorial representations (e.g., have students make prefix word cards with words on one side and sketches on the other—these can be used to play word games or as independent study aids).

- **Tier III:** Coordinate with the student's tutor or special education teacher. Allow extra time. Provide extra opportunities for practice and review. Individual instruction may be needed. Monitor progress more often than with Tier II students.

How to Use This Book

This introductory section of *Starting with Prefixes and Suffixes* presents management, research, and background information to orient you to a roots approach. *Starting with Prefixes and Suffixes* is a stand-alone resource for teachers and students that presents the most frequently encountered prefixes and suffixes in English. Each lesson provides content explanations, instructional guidelines, and student activities necessary to teach prefixes and suffixes and help learners understand how to "dissect" (Divide and Conquer) and "compose" (Combine and Create) words from everyday and academic vocabulary. Suggestions for extension activities and assessment are also included (see Appendix B).

The first two lessons are about compound words. These lessons help students learn how and why to dissect long words for meaning-bearing units. Five instructional units present multiple lessons, four of which are followed by a Review Page (suitable for assessment). Unit 1 focuses on compound words. Units 2–4 focus on prefixes. Unit 5 focuses on suffixes.

Instructional Planning

Before beginning to teach with *Starting with Prefixes and Suffixes*, read the introductory material and skim several lessons. Then, decide how to incorporate the lessons within your reading/language arts curriculum:

- How many minutes per day can you devote to the lessons?

- How often can you teach them during the week?

- At what time of day will you and your students practice with prefixes and suffixes?

- Glance at the Review Page at the end of Units 2–5, which can be used for assessment.

How to Use This Book *(cont.)*

The information in this book is cumulative but not sequential. Depending on your students, you may begin at any point. The following is a brief description of each unit.

Unit I introduces the strategy of examining words for semantic units (i.e., parts that have meaning and not merely sound) and introduces the Divide and Conquer strategy. Simple two- and three-syllable compound words are the focus of these lessons. Unit II presents common negative prefixes: *un-*, *in-* (and assimilated forms, *im-* and *il-*), and *dis-*. Unit III introduces common directional prefixes: *re-*, *pre-*, *ex-*, *sub-*, *de-*, and *co-/con-*. Unit IV presents numerical and quantitative prefixes: *uni-/unit-*, *bi-*, *tri-*, *quart-/quadr-*, and *multi-*. Unit V introduces several common suffixes: *-less*, *-ful*, *-er*, *-est*, and *-ly*. To the extent possible, examples are included that show prefixes and suffixes attached to intact words.

About Unit I

Unit I introduces students to the skill of "dividing and conquering" vocabulary. Lessons 1 and 2 present easy and familiar compound words. By dividing compound words into component parts, students learn to look inside a word for its semantic units (i.e., parts that have meaning and not merely sound).

About Unit II

Unit II presents the most common negative prefixes in the English vocabulary. Lessons 3 and 4 continue to build on the skill of looking inside a word for its semantic unit while focusing on the prefixes *un-* and *in-*. Lesson 5 introduces the concept of assimilation: the prefix *in-*, ending in a consonant, changes into *im-* or *il-*, depending on the following consonant in the word (e.g., *impossible, illegal*). Lesson 6 introduces the negative prefix *dis-*, which means "not." The prefix occurs in many academic words and can negate whole words. The majority of the sample words presents prefixes attached to intact words. Students will learn how to negate an existing word as well as how to detach a negating prefix and recognize the original word. The Combine and Create activities and the Read and Reason passages present the prefixes and words in larger contexts. The unit ends with a one-page review exercise suitable for assessment.

About Unit III

Unit III presents more of the most useful directional prefixes: *re-*, *pre-*, *ex-*, *sub-*, *de-*, and *co-/con-*. Lesson 7, for example, addresses the prefixes *re-* ("back, again") and Lesson 8 addresses the prefix *pre-* ("before"), which attach to intact words and to Latin bases. They form many words that students either already know or will readily recognize. Lesson 9 presents the prefix *ex-*, which means "out," and Lesson 10 presents *sub-*, meaning "under" or "below." Lesson 11 presents *de-*, meaning "down, off of," in such everyday words as *defrost* and in academic words like *deflate, descend,* and *demolish*. Lesson 12 presents the prefixes *co-* and *con-*, explaining that the form *co-* frequently attaches to intact words (e.g., *coauthor, costar, coworker*) and that *con-* attaches to many Latin bases (e.g., *convert, conduct, contact*).

How to Use This Book *(cont.)*

About Unit IV

Unit IV presents some of the most frequently occurring numerical prefixes: *uni-* and *unit-*, *bi-*, *tri-*, *quart-* and *quadr-*, and *multi-*. The numerical prefixes *uni-* and *unit-*, presented in Lesson 13, appear in many words that students readily recognize as meaning "one": a *unicorn* has "one" horn; a *unicycle* has "one" wheel. But this prefix appears in other words that students may never have thought about as meaning "one": a *uniform* is a "single" "form" of clothing worn by many people; a *unique* person is "one of a kind, singular." Lesson 14 presents the numerical prefix *bi-*, meaning "two," while Lesson 15 discusses the prefix *tri-*, meaning "three." In addition to appearing in common words (e.g., *bicycle, triangle*), these prefixes appear in specialized academic words (e.g., *bilateral agreements, bicameral congress, trisected angles*). Lesson 16 discusses *quart-* and *quadr-*, numerical prefixes meaning "four" or "one-fourth." These numerical prefixes are found particularly in mathematics, but they appear in other content areas as well. Lesson 17 presents the Latin prefix *multi-*, meaning "many," which appears in academic words (e.g., a *multilingual* person speaks "many" "languages"; a *multilateral* agreement reflects the "many" "sides" of the parties agreeing to it).

About Unit V

Unit V marks the beginning of the study of suffixes. Until this point, students have been developing and building upon their knowledge of prefixes and base words, giving limited attention to the suffixes that attach to the ends of whole words and word parts. By doing so, they are building the foundation necessary for launching their study of suffixes, starting with the suffix *-less*, meaning "without," which is presented in Lesson 18. However, students come to understand that both prefixes and suffixes serve a similar purpose; they change the meaning of the base word. Lesson 19 introduces the suffix *-ful*, meaning "full of," followed by the suffix *-er*, meaning "more," presented in Lesson 20, followed by the suffix *-est*, meaning "most," presented in Lesson 21. Students discover that these suffixes (*-er* and *-est*) inherently compare two or more things: *big, bigger, biggest*. Unit V closes with the suffix *-ly*, meaning "in a _____ way," which explains the significance of *-ly* in relation to actions. Each lesson in Unit V includes Spelling Tips for teachers to impart to students, providing students with the appropriate spelling rules when adding suffixes to words.

How to Use This Book *(cont.)*

Lesson Overview

Each lesson begins with **Teaching Tips** that provide essential information about the prefix. Reading this section before you teach the lesson will provide you with a foundation to ensure student success.

The **Guided Practice** portion of each lesson includes suggestions for **Activating Background Knowledge** about the prefix or suffix. These suggestions provide interactive teaching strategies to help elicit what students already know and to build on that foundation.

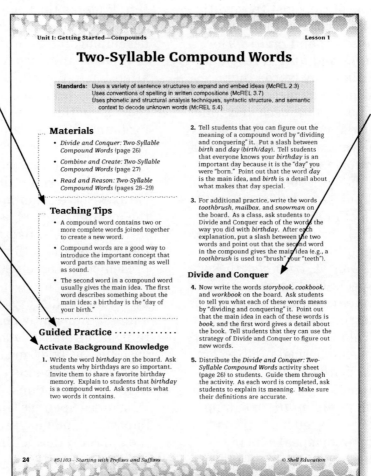

Then students are presented with a word list called **Divide and Conquer**. Each word includes the prefix or suffix that is the focus of the lesson. The prefixes or suffixes are attached to both intact English words and to Latin bases, whose meaning is provided. As students "translate" the prefix or suffix and the base word, they study the meaning of each semantic unit and identify the definition from the Answer Bank. This activity helps students understand how to extract meaning using roots.

How to Use This Book *(cont.)*

The **Combine and Create** activity of each lesson teaches students to combine word parts in order to use words in written and oral academic work. In these activities, students combine word parts (prefixes, suffixes, and bases) to generate vocabulary, and they also examine context clues (for words in phrases and textbook settings, including short composition sentences) to determine correct responses. As students complete and review their answers, they share the words and sentences they have made with classmates because using and hearing new words is an important part of learning them.

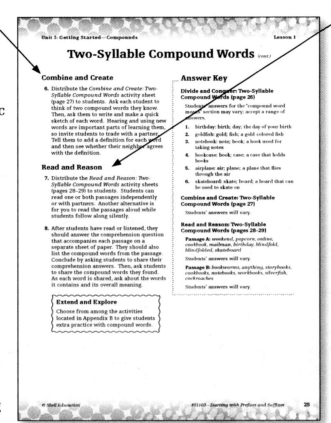

Two **Read and Reason** activities follow, one at an easy readability level and one more challenging. You may choose one or both of these passages, which contain several words using the prefix or suffix of the lesson. As students read to themselves or listen to the teacher reading aloud, they identify the prefix or suffix words in extended texts that center on a wide range of interesting topics.

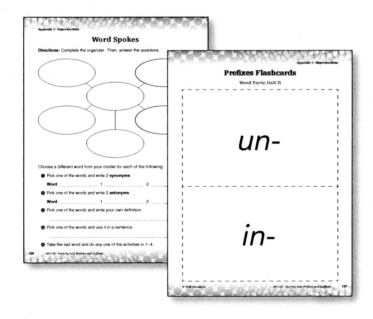

If additional practice is needed or desired, you may use the **Extend and Explore** activities found in the Digital Resources (extendexplore.pdf).

How to Use This Book (cont.)

Tips for Implementation

In this section, we offer some general implementation tips as well as extension ideas.

General Tips

As you plan, keep instructional goals and learning outcomes in mind. Develop regular routines for vocabulary instruction and practice. Read the **Teaching Tips** before beginning each lesson.

Some teachers have noticed a "learning curve" when their students begin working from a roots approach, perhaps because students are accustomed to memorizing only as a word-learning strategy. Be patient with your students while they are experiencing this learning curve; provide extra support if needed (e.g., invite students to work in pairs).

When you introduce a new prefix or suffix, do the dividing and conquering with students before asking them to work independently. Encourage students to work with partners so they can talk through the process. Also, find time for students to explore words with others. When discussing answers, use the definition of the root in your talk (e.g., *replay* means "play again"). You can also reword key sentences by substituting the root meaning for the word. Remember to keep the focus on the meanings of the prefixes or suffixes and not on memorizing particular words.

If students have questions about words that you cannot answer, you can say, "I'm not sure. Let's look it up." Then, show students how to consult a reference resource to find the answer. Do not shy away from using this option. It is important for students to understand that word learning is a lifelong process and that teachers are learners, too. Moreover, these situations provide authentic opportunities to teach students how to use reference books and websites.

Above all, we urge you to create a classroom setting that stimulates word curiosity and exploration. Consider using the prefix or suffix you are teaching as a "Root of the Week." Encourage students to search for words that share the prefix or suffix and add them to a list you have prominently displayed in the classroom. Whenever possible, encourage playful activities where students can explore words with the prefix or suffix they are studying. Such activities can often be quick and spontaneous. If you have a few extra moments, try 20 Questions or play Hangman with a word that uses the prefix or suffix students are learning.

Extension Possibilities

Students might complete some activities in learning centers, workstations, or as homework. The Combine and Create and Read and Reason sections of each lesson may work especially well for this purpose. Consider using the Read and Reason passages for fluency practice. Make word walls featuring prefixes or suffixes you are studying. Invite students to look for words containing the prefix or suffix to add to the word wall. Challenge students to use these words in their writing (and oral language as well).

Ask students to review their previous writing for examples of words with the prefix or suffix of focus. These could be placed on a large sheet of chart paper or added to the word wall.

Challenge students to use words with prefixes or suffixes in their content-area study. They can look for words containing a prefix or suffix in their reading and, perhaps, post these on chart paper. If enough words are accumulated, students can develop webs showing how the words relate to the content-area topic of study.

Correlation to Standards

Shell Education is committed to producing educational materials that are research and standards based. In this effort, we have correlated all of our products to the academic standards of all 50 United States, the District of Columbia, the Department of Defense Dependent Schools, and all Canadian provinces.

How to Find Standards Correlations

To print a customized correlation report of this product for your state, visit our website at http://www.shelleducation.com and follow the on-screen directions. If you require assistance in printing correlation reports, please contact Customer Service at 1-800-858-7339.

Purpose and Intent of Standards

Legislation mandates that all states adopt academic standards that identify the skills students will learn in kindergarten through grade twelve. Many states also have standards for Pre-K. This same legislation sets requirements to ensure the standards are detailed and comprehensive.

Standards are designed to focus instruction and guide adoption of curricula. Standards are statements that describe the criteria necessary for students to meet specific academic goals. They define the knowledge, skills, and content students should acquire at each level. Standards are also used to develop standardized tests to evaluate students' academic progress.

Teachers are required to demonstrate how their lessons meet state standards. State standards are used in the development of all of our products, so educators can be assured they meet the academic requirements of each state.

McREL Compendium

We use the Mid-continent Research for Education and Learning (McREL) Compendium to create standards correlations. Each year, McREL analyzes state standards and revises the compendium. By following this procedure, McREL is able to produce a general compilation of national standards. Each lesson in this product is based on one or more McREL standards. The chart on the following page and in the Digital Resources (mcrel.pdf) lists each standard taught in this product and the page numbers for the corresponding lessons.

Common Core State Standards

The lessons in this book are aligned to the Common Core State Standards (CCSS). The standards correlation can be found in the Digital Resources (ccss.pdf).

TESOL and WIDA Standards

The lessons in this book promote English language development for English language learners. The standards correlation can be found in the Digital Resources (tesolwida.pdf).

Correlation to Standards (cont.)

McREL Standards

Standard	Page(s)
2.3—Uses a variety of sentence structures to expand and embed ideas	24, 30, 36, 42, 48, 54, 61, 67, 73, 79, 85, 91, 100, 107, 113, 119, 125, 133, 140, 146, 153, 159
3.7—Uses conventions of spelling in written compositions	24, 30, 36, 42, 48, 54, 61, 67, 73, 79, 85, 91, 100, 107, 113, 119, 125, 133, 140, 146, 153, 159
5.4—Uses phonetic and structural analysis techniques, syntactic structure, and semantic context to decode unknown words	24, 30, 36, 42, 48, 54, 61, 67, 73, 79, 85, 91, 100, 107, 113, 119, 125, 133, 140, 146, 153, 159

Correlation to Standards *(cont.)*

Common Core State Standards

One of the main focuses of the Common Core State Standards is to "help ensure that all students are college and career ready in literacy no later than the end of high school." As such, the lessons presented in this book support this effort by helping develop students' literacy skills through the study of prefixes and suffixes.

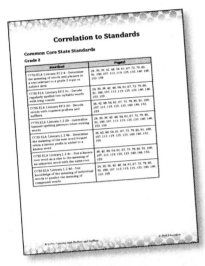
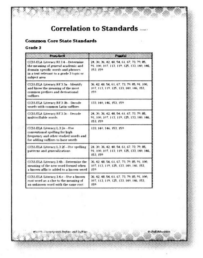
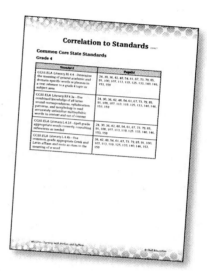

TESOL and WIDA Standards

The lessons in this book promote English language development for English language learners. The standards can be found in the Digital Resources.

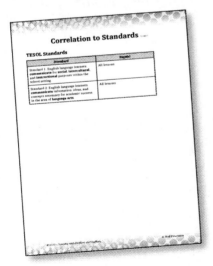
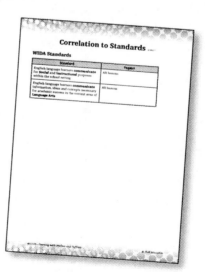

About the Authors

Timothy Rasinski, Ph.D., is a professor of literacy education at Kent State University. He has written over 150 articles and has authored, coauthored, or edited more than 15 books and curriculum programs on reading education. His research on reading has been cited by the National Reading Panel and has been published in journals such as *Reading Research Quarterly, The Reading Teacher, Reading Psychology*, and *The Journal of Educational Research*. Tim served on the Board of Directors of the International Reading Association, and from 1992–1999, he was coeditor of *The Reading Teacher*, the world's most widely read journal of literacy education. He has also served as editor of the *Journal of Literacy Research*, one of the premier research journals in reading. Tim is a past president of the College Reading Association, and he has won the A.B. Herr Award from the College Reading Association for his scholarly contributions to literacy education.

Nancy Padak, Ed.D., is an active researcher, author, and consultant. She was a Distinguished Professor in the College and Graduate School of Education, Health, and Human Services at Kent State University. She directed KSU's Reading and Writing Center and taught in the area of literacy education. She was the Principal Investigator for the Ohio Literacy Resource Center, which has provided support for adult and family literacy programs since 1993. Prior to her arrival at Kent State in 1985, she was a classroom teacher and district administrator. She has written or edited more than 25 books and more than 90 chapters and articles. She has also served in a variety of leadership roles in professional organizations, including the presidency of the College Reading Association and (with others) the editor of *The Reading Teacher* and the *Journal of Literacy Research.* She has won several awards for her scholarship and contributions to literacy education.

About the Authors *(cont.)*

Rick M. Newton, Ph.D., holds a doctoral degree in Greek and Latin from the University of Michigan and is now an emeritus professor of Greek and Latin at Kent State University. He developed the course "English Words from Classical Elements," which more than 15,000 Kent State students have taken over the past 30 years. He holds the Distinguished Teaching Award from the Kent State College of Arts and Sciences and the Translation Award from the Modern Greek Studies Association of North America and Canada.

Evangeline Newton, Ph.D., is a professor of literacy education at the University of Akron where she served as the first director of the Center for Literacy. She teaches a variety of literacy methods courses and professional development workshops to elementary, middle, and high school teachers. A former coeditor of *The Ohio Reading Teacher*, Evangeline currently chairs the Reading Review Board of the Ohio Resource Center for Mathematics, Science, and Reading. She serves on editorial review boards for *The Reading Teacher* and *Reading Horizons*. Evangeline is active in the Association of Literacy Educators and the International Reading Association (IRA). As a participant in IRA's Reading and Writing for Critical Thinking project, Evangeline taught workshops for teachers and Peace Corps volunteers in Armenia. A former St. Louis public school teacher, Evangeline holds a B.A. from Washington University in St. Louis, an M.A.T. from Webster University, and a Ph.D. from Kent State University.

Two-Syllable Compound Words

> **Standards:** Uses a variety of sentence structures to expand and embed ideas (McREL 2.3)
> Uses conventions of spelling in written compositions (McREL 3.7)
> Uses phonetic and structural analysis techniques, syntactic structure, and semantic context to decode unknown words (McREL 5.4)

Materials

- *Divide and Conquer: Two-Syllable Compound Words* (page 26)

- *Combine and Create: Two-Syllable Compound Words* (page 27)

- *Read and Reason: Two-Syllable Compound Words* (pages 28–29)

Teaching Tips

- A compound word contains two or more complete words joined together to create a new word.

- Compound words are a good way to introduce the important concept that word parts can have meaning as well as sound.

- The second word in a compound word usually gives the main idea. The first word describes something about the main idea: a birthday is the "day of your birth."

Guided Practice · · · · · · · · · · · ·

Activate Background Knowledge

1. Write the word *birthday* on the board. Ask students why birthdays are so important. Invite them to share a favorite birthday memory. Explain to students that *birthday* is a compound word. Ask students what two words it contains.

2. Tell students that you can figure out the meaning of a compound word by "dividing and conquering" it. Put a slash between *birth* and *day* (*birth/day*). Tell students that everyone knows your *birthday* is an important day because it is the "day" you were "born." Point out that the word *day* is the main idea, and *birth* is a detail about what makes that day special.

3. For additional practice, write the words *toothbrush, mailbox,* and *snowman* on the board. As a class, ask students to Divide and Conquer each of the words the way you did with *birthday*. After each explanation, put a slash between the two words and point out that the second word in the compound gives the main idea (e.g., a *toothbrush* is used to "brush" your "teeth").

Divide and Conquer

4. Now write the words *storybook, cookbook,* and *workbook* on the board. Ask students to tell you what each of these words means by "dividing and conquering" it. Point out that the main idea in each of these words is *book,* and the first word gives a detail about the book. Tell students that they can use the strategy of Divide and Conquer to figure out new words.

5. Distribute the *Divide and Conquer: Two-Syllable Compound Words* activity sheet (page 26) to students. Guide them through the activity. As each word is completed, ask students to explain its meaning. Make sure their definitions are accurate.

Two-Syllable Compound Words *(cont.)*

Combine and Create

6. Distribute the *Combine and Create: Two-Syllable Compound Words* activity sheet (page 27) to students. Ask each student to think of two compound words they know. Then, ask them to write and make a quick sketch of each word. Hearing and using new words are important parts of learning them, so invite students to trade with a partner. Tell them to add a definition for each word and then see whether their neighbor agrees with the definition.

Read and Reason

7. Distribute the *Read and Reason: Two-Syllable Compound Words* activity sheets (pages 28–29) to students. Students can read one or both passages independently or with partners. Another alternative is for you to read the passages aloud while students follow along silently.

8. After students have read or listened, they should answer the comprehension question that accompanies each passage on a separate sheet of paper. They should also list the compound words from the passage. Conclude by asking students to share their comprehension answers. Then, ask students to share the compound words they found. As each word is shared, ask about the words it contains and its overall meaning.

Extend and Explore

Choose from among the activities located in Appendix B to give students extra practice with compound words.

Answer Key

Divide and Conquer: Two-Syllable Compound Words (page 26)

Students' answers for the "compound word means" section may vary; accept a range of answers.

1. birthday: birth; day; the day of your birth
2. goldfish: gold; fish; a gold-colored fish
3. notebook: note; book; a book used for taking notes
4. bookcase: book; case; a case that holds books
5. airplane: air; plane; a plane that flies through the air
6. skateboard: skate; board; a board that can be used to skate on

Combine and Create: Two-Syllable Compound Words (page 27)

Students' answers will vary.

Read and Reason: Two-Syllable Compound Words (pages 28–29)

Passage A: *weekend, popcorn, online, cookbook, mailman, birthday, blindfold, blindfolded, skateboard*

Students' answers will vary.

Passage B: *bookworms, anything, storybooks, cookbooks, notebooks, workbooks, silverfish, cockroaches*

Students' answers will vary.

Name: _____ Date: _____

Divide and Conquer:
Two-Syllable Compound Words

Directions: Break apart each compound word. Write a simple definition for each word. An example has been done for you.

compound word	base word	base word	compound word means
1 birthday	birth	day	the day of your birth
2 goldfish			
3 notebook			
4 bookcase			
5 airplane			
6 skateboard			

Name: _____ Date: _____

Combine and Create:
Two-Syllable Compound Words

Directions: Think of two compound words. Write the word and then draw a sketch of it.

❶ _____	❷ _____

Directions: Now trade papers with a friend. Read each word, look at the sketch, and then write your own definition. Return the paper and see if your partner agrees with you.

❶ _____ means	❷ _____ means
_____	_____
_____	_____
_____	_____
_____	_____
_____	_____
_____	_____

Name: _____   Date: _____

Read and Reason:
Two-Syllable Compound Words

Directions: Read the passage. Circle the compound words. Then, answer the questions.

Passage A

Hooray for Birthdays!

Last weekend, I turned 10. "Two digits," my mom said. "This is a big deal!" My family helped me have fun.

I like popcorn. We decided to look at an online cookbook to find new tastes for popcorn. We made five kinds! We made candy bar popcorn, peanut butter popcorn, nutty popcorn, and caramel popcorn balls. The fifth kind? Regular popcorn. Yum!

The mailman came to deliver birthday cards while we were making popcorn. I got a couple of birthday cards. I also got a mysterious note from my aunt. It said, "Your dad will put a blindfold on you. You will go with him in the car. At the end of the ride, you will see my birthday present for you." So my dad blindfolded me, and we left in the car. The car stopped at a sports store. We went inside and there it was—a brand new skateboard with a big red bow on it. I was surprised!

My 10th birthday was so much fun. I wonder what my family will do when I turn 11!

Which kind of popcorn from the story would you like to eat? Why?

Name: _____ Date: _____

Read and Reason:
Two-Syllable Compound Words *(cont.)*

Directions: Read the passage. Circle the compound words. Then, answer the question.

Passage B

Are You a Bookworm?

There are two kinds of bookworms. One is a person. The other is an insect.

People who are bookworms love to read. They read all the time. Some bookworms will read almost anything. They will read storybooks, cookbooks, notebooks, or even workbooks!

Bookworms can also be insects that like to eat books. They like the taste of the glue that holds books together. They also like to eat the paper in books. Some beetles are bookworms. Other bookworms are silverfish and cockroaches.

Are you a bookworm? Tell how you are or are not.

Three-Syllable Compound Words

> **Standards:** Uses a variety of sentence structures to expand and embed ideas (McREL 2.3)
> Uses conventions of spelling in written compositions (McREL 3.7)
> Uses phonetic and structural analysis techniques, syntactic structure, and semantic context to decode unknown words (McREL 5.4)

Materials

- *Divide and Conquer: Three-Syllable Compound Words* (page 32)
- *Combine and Create: Three-Syllable Compound Words* (page 33)
- *Read and Reason: Three-Syllable Compound Words* (pages 34–35)

Teaching Tips

- A compound word contains two or more complete words joined together to create a new word. Because they contain three syllables but only two meaning units, three-syllable compound words are a good way to show students that meaning units can be bigger than one syllable. *Fingernail*, for example, has three syllables (*fing/er/nail*) but only two meaning units (*finger/nail*).

- Remind students that the second word in a compound word usually tells the main idea. The first word describes something about the main idea: a *firefighter* is someone who "fights" "fires"; a *fingernail* is a "nail" on the "finger."

Guided Practice

Activate Background Knowledge

1. Write the words *weekend* and *grandmother* on the board. Working in pairs, have students pick one of the words and explain its meaning. You may want to invite them to share any favorite weekend or grandmother memories. Point out that while both *weekend* and *grandmother* are compound words, *weekend* only has two syllables while *grandmother* has three.

2. Remind students that you can figure out the meaning of compound words by "dividing and conquering" them. Put a slash between each semantic unit in the compound words (*week/end; grand/mother*). Tell students that when they Divide and Conquer compound words, they need to look for whole words (units of meaning) and not syllables (units of sound). Point out that they could not figure out the meaning of "grandmother" if they divided the word by syllables (*grand/moth/er*) instead of meaning (*grand/mother*).

3. Remind them that the second word in the compound word tells the main idea (e.g., a *grandmother* is a "mother" who is "grand" because she is special).

4. Now make a list that includes both two- and three-syllable words (e.g., *eyelid, beehive, honeybee, mailbox, loudspeaker, waterfall*). Ask student volunteers to Divide and Conquer by selecting a word and telling what two words it contains. Point out that some of them have two syllables and some have three syllables. Remind students that when dividing words into parts, they should look for word parts that have meaning.

Three-Syllable Compound Words *(cont.)*

Divide and Conquer

5. Distribute the *Divide and Conquer: Three-Syllable Compound Words* activity sheet (page 32) to students. Guide them through the activity. As each word is completed, ask students to explain its meaning. Make sure their definitions are accurate.

Combine and Create

6. Distribute the *Combine and Create: Three-Syllable Compound Words* activity sheet (page 33) to students. Ask each student to make six compound words by matching a word in Box A with a word in Box B. After they write each of the new words, tell students to write two sentences using some of the words. Hearing and using new words are important parts of learning them, so make sure students share the sentences they made with classmates.

Read and Reason

7. Distribute the *Read and Reason: Three-Syllable Compound Words* activity sheets (pages 34–35) to students. Have students read one or both passages and answer the comprehension questions on a separate sheet of paper. Ask students to circle the compound words they find. If the passages are too difficult for independent reading, ask students to read in pairs or follow along as you read aloud. If you read the passage to them, tell them to raise their hands when they hear a compound word of two or more syllables. After they (or you) have finished reading, discuss the passage. Ask student volunteers to identify compound words and explain what they mean.

Extend and Explore

Choose from among the activities located in Appendix B to give students extra practice with compound words.

Answer Key

Divide and Conquer: Three-Syllable Compound Words (page 32)

Students' answers for the "compound word means" section may vary; accept a range of answers.

1. firefighter: fire; fighter; a person who fights fires
2. thunderstorm: thunder; storm; a storm with thunder
3. flowerpot: flower; pot; a pot for flowers or plants
4. grandparent: grand; parent; a parent who is older/grander (in years) than a parent
5. honeybee: honey; bee; a bee that makes honey
6. blackberry: black; berry; a berry that is black

Combine and Create: Three-Syllable Compound Words (page 33)

afternoon, candlestick, grandchildren, honeycomb, thunderstorm, waterfall

Students' answers will vary.

Read and Reason: Three-Syllable Compound Words (pages 34–35)

Passage A: *blueberry, strawberry, honeybees, honeycombs, underground, rainwater, thunderstorm*

Students' answers will vary.

Passage B: *superhero, Superheroes, superheroes, superpowers, Superwoman, skyscraper, superhuman, waterproof, sunscreen, summertime, waterski, sandcastles, Aquaboy's, Aquaboy, underwater*

Students' answers will vary.

Name: _____ Date: _____

Divide and Conquer:
Three-Syllable Compound Words

Directions: Break apart each compound word. Write a simple definition for each word. An example has been done for you.

compound word	base word	base word	compound word means
1 firefighter	fire	fighter	a person who fights fires
2 thunderstorm			
3 flowerpot			
4 grandparent			
5 honeybee			
6 blackberry			

Name: _____   Date: _____

Combine and Create:
Combine and Create:
Three-Syllable Compound Words

Directions: Form six compound words by combining the words in the columns. Combine each word in Column A with a word from Column B to create compound words that make sense.

Box A (first part of the word)		Box B (second part of the word)	
candle	after	children	storm
grand	thunder	comb	noon
honey	water	stick	fall

My compound words are:

_____   _____

_____   _____

_____   _____

Now, write two sentences using two of the compound words you made.

_____

_____

_____

_____

_____

Name: _____   Date: _____

Read and Reason:
Three-Syllable Compound Words

Directions: Read the passage. Circle the compound words. Then, answer the question.

Passage A

Bonnie's Farm

My friend Bonnie bought a small farm. She planted blueberry bushes and strawberry plants. She planted potatoes, other vegetables, and seeds for flowers.

She also has honeybees. They live in two hives. They make honeycombs. They get nectar from the blueberry bushes, strawberry plants, and flowers. They will use the nectar to make honey.

Bonnie had a problem. She needed water for her farm. The plants need water to grow. Even the bees need water! She dug a well to pump water from deep underground. She also has a barrel to catch rainwater. After a thunderstorm, she uses the rainwater for her bees and plants.

What do you think Bonnie will do with her fruit, vegetables, and honey?

Name: _____ Date: _____

Read and Reason:
Three-Syllable Compound Words (cont.)

Directions: Read the passage. Circle the compound words. Then, answer the question.

Passage B

Superheroes

Have you ever pretended to be a superhero? Superheroes got their start in comic books. Now they also appear on TV and in movies. All superheroes have superpowers.

Superwoman wears a cape and has a big *S* on her uniform. She can fly. She can also jump very high, even over a skyscraper! She has superhuman strength.

Sun Girl uses the Sun's rays to melt ice on cold days. She always wears waterproof sunscreen. During the summertime, she uses her powers to warm beaches. Then, kids can waterski or build sandcastles!

What do you think Aquaboy's superpowers are? If you guessed something to do with water, you're right! Aquaboy can breathe underwater. He can also communicate with ocean creatures.

All superheroes have superpowers. And all of them fight evil. Wouldn't it be nice if they were real?

> Which superhero would you like to be? Tell why.

Negative Prefix *un-*

Standards: Uses a variety of sentence structures to expand and embed ideas (McREL 2.3)
Uses conventions of spelling in written compositions (McREL 3.7)
Uses phonetic and structural analysis techniques, syntactic structure, and semantic context to decode unknown words (McREL 5.4)

Materials

- *Divide and Conquer: Negative Prefix un-* (page 38)

- *Combine and Create: Negative Prefix un-* (page 39)

- *Read and Reason: Negative Prefix un-* (pages 40–41)

Teaching Tips

- *Un-* is the most common prefix in English. It means "not."

- A *prefix* is a unit of meaning that comes at the beginning of a word. It describes something about the main idea: An *unzipped* jacket is "not" "zipped."

- A *base* is a unit of meaning that gives the main idea. It can be a whole word or a word part. *Un-* usually attaches to bases that are whole words.

Guided Practice · · · · · · · · · · · ·

Activate Background Knowledge

1. Introduce or review the concept that a prefix is a unit of meaning that comes at the beginning of a word. Write the word *happy* on the board. Ask students to think of something that makes them happy. Now add the prefix *un-* to the word happy. Ask students to talk about how adding *un-* to the word changed its meaning. Put a slash after *un-*. Tell students the prefix *un-* means "not."

2. Remind students that you can figure out the meaning of new words by dividing and conquering them. Write the words *zipped*, *tied,* and *buttoned* on the board. Put a slash between *un-* and the base word (*un/zipped; un/tied; un/buttoned*). Working with partners or as a whole class, ask students to explain how adding the prefix *un-* changed each of these words (e.g., *unzipped* = "not" "zipped"; *untied* = "not" "tied"; *unbuttoned* = "not" "buttoned").

3. For extra practice, invite students to brainstorm more *un-* words they know. Invite them to choose a word on the list and tell a neighbor how *un-* changed its meaning. You can display the list as a word wall for use in different activities.

Divide and Conquer

4. Distribute the *Divide and Conquer: Negative Prefix un-* activity sheet (page 38) to students. Guide them through the activity. As each word is completed, ask students to explain what it means. Make sure their definitions make sense.

Negative Prefix *un-* (cont.)

Combine and Create

5. Distribute the *Combine and Create: Negative Prefix un-* activity sheet (page 39) to students. Ask students to add the prefix *un-* to the base words provided. Working independently or with a partner, ask students to write a story using all of the *un-* words they have made. Using and hearing new words is an important part of learning them, so make sure students share the stories they have written.

Read and Reason

6. Distribute the *Read and Reason: Negative Prefix un-* activity sheets (pages 40–41) to students. Have students read one or both passages and answer the comprehension questions on a separate sheet of paper. Ask students to circle the *un-* words they find. If the passages are too difficult for independent reading, ask students to read in pairs or follow along as you read aloud. If you read the passage to them, tell them to raise their hands when they hear an *un-* word. After they (or you) have finished reading, discuss the passage. Ask volunteers to identify *un-* words and explain what they mean.

Extend and Explore

Choose from among the activities located in Appendix B to give students extra practice with *un-* words.

Answer Key

Divide and Conquer: Negative Prefix *un-* (page 38)

Students' answers for the "definition" section may vary; accept a range of answers.

1. unhealthy: not; healthy; not healthy
2. unsafe: not; safe; not safe
3. unfriendly: not; friendly; not friendly
4. unlucky: not; lucky; not lucky
5. untrue: not; true; not true
6. unsure: not; sure; not sure

Combine and Create: Negative Prefix *un-* (page 39)

1. unwrap
2. unlucky
3. untidy
4. uncertain
5. unpack
6. unlock

Students' stories will vary.

Read and Reason: Negative Prefix *un-* (pages 40–41)

Passage A: *Untie, Unlatch, Unbundle, Unlock*

Students' answers will vary.

Passage B: *unsafe, unlucky, unsure, unexpected*

Students' answers will vary.

Name: _____ Date: _____

Divide and Conquer:
Negative Prefix *un-*

Directions: Break apart each word. Write the prefix and its meaning, the base word, and a simple definition for each word. An example has been done for you.

word	prefix means	base word	definition
❶ unhealthy	*un-* = not	healthy	not healthy
❷ unsafe			
❸ unfriendly			
❹ unlucky			
❺ untrue			
❻ unsure			

Name: _____   Date: _____

Combine and Create:
Negative Prefix *un-*

Directions: Add *un-* to each of the words. Then, write a story using as many of these new *un-* words as you can. Make sure to give your story a title.

❶ wrap _____   **❹** certain _____

❷ lucky _____   **❺** pack _____

❸ tidy _____   **❻** lock _____

My Story

_____

_____

_____

_____

_____

_____

_____

_____

_____

Name: _____   Date: _____

Read and Reason:
Negative Prefix _un-_

Directions: Read the passage. Circle the words with the prefix _un-_. Then, answer the question.

Passage A

One, Two

One, two

Untie your shoe

Three, four

Unlatch the door

Five, six

Unbundle the sticks

Seven, eight

Unlock the crate

Nine, ten

Do it again!

Rewrite the poem without the prefix _un-_. How does the meaning change?

Name: _____   Date: _____

Read and Reason:
Negative Prefix *un-* (cont.)

Directions: Read the passage. Circle the words with the prefix *un-*. Then, answer the questions.

Passage B

An Unlucky Day?

What do you think about Friday the 13th? Do you feel unsafe on this day or not? Do you think it is an unlucky day? Or are you unsure?

As many as 20 million people in the United States think that Friday the 13th is an unlucky day. Some people are afraid to fly on this day. Others do not even go to work. These people fear unexpected accidents. So they stay home.

Many hotels do not have 13th floors. Many people think the number 13 is unlucky. Maybe this is why Friday the 13th became unlucky. We're really not sure.

Do you think Friday the 13th is an unlucky day? Why or why not?

Negative Prefix *in-*

Standards: Uses a variety of sentence structures to expand and embed ideas (McREL 2.3)
Uses conventions of spelling in written compositions (McREL 3.7)
Uses phonetic and structural analysis techniques, syntactic structure, and semantic context to decode unknown words (McREL 5.4)

Materials

- *Divide and Conquer: Negative Prefix in-* (page 44)
- *Combine and Create: Negative Prefix in-* (page 45)
- *Read and Reason: Negative Prefix in-* (pages 46–47)

Teaching Tips

- The English language has two prefixes (*in-*) that are spelled alike but mean different things. This lesson focuses on the negative prefix *in-*. The negative prefix *in-* means "not" in words like *invisible* ("not" visible) and *incomplete* ("not" complete). The other prefix *in-* is directional, meaning "in, on, into." It appears in words like *inhabit* (to live "in" an area). The prefix *in-* can undergo assimilation (see pages 6–8) and appear as *im-, il-*. The assimilated forms *im-, il-* are presented in Lesson 5.

- The prefix *in-* attaches to both whole words and word parts (e.g., the adjective *incapable* is the negative form of *capable*; the word *intact*, meaning "whole, not broken," begins with the prefix *in-*, which is attached to a Latin base *tact-*, which means "touched"). Something *intact* is whole and unbroken because it is "not" (*in-*) "touched" (*tact-*). The prefix *in-* in this lesson attaches to whole words only.

Guided Practice · · · · · · · · · · · ·

Activate Background Knowledge

1. Review the concept of a *prefix* (a unit added to the front of a word that influences its meaning). Explain that *in-* is a prefix meaning "not." It changes the meaning of the word to something negative. Write the words *correct* and *visible* on the board. Point out that both of these words have meanings that can be changed into a negative with *in-*. Then, add *in-* to both words.

2. Working with partners or as a whole class, ask students to determine what the new words mean. Then, ask them to explain how the prefix changes the meaning (e.g., *incorrect* means "not" "correct"; *invisible* means "not" "visible"). Adding *in-* makes the original word negative.

3. Write the word *appropriate* on the board. Ask students to generate a list of behaviors that are appropriate at school. Then, add the prefix *in-* to the word *appropriate*. Invite students to brainstorm a list of behaviors that are inappropriate at school. Draw students' attention to how the prefix *in-* changes the meaning of *appropriate* from positive (acceptable school behaviors) to negative (behaviors that are not acceptable). Ask students to generate more *in-* words they know and explain how adding *in-* changes the meaning of the word.

Negative Prefix *in-* *(cont.)*

4. However, *in-* does not always mean "not," just like *re-* does not always means "back or again" (e.g., the *re-* in read). Emphasize the importance of considering the meaning of the word and its context when determining whether *in-* means "not." For example, where is the negative prefix *in-* in the words *inspire* and *into*? Having continued discussions about word meanings is an effective way to build students' word analysis skills as well as their capacity to use context clues.

Divide and Conquer

5. Distribute the *Divide and Conquer: Negative Prefix in-* activity sheet (page 44) to students. Guide students through the activity sheet. As each word is completed, ask students to explain its meaning. Make sure their definitions are accurate.

Combine and Create

6. Distribute the *Combine and Create: Negative Prefix in-* activity sheet (page 45) to students. Ask students to work in pairs to generate new words by adding the prefix *in-* to known base words. Have students draw pictures of the *in-* words they create. Visually depicting words that represent abstract concepts helps students develop their understanding of those words. Make sure students have an opportunity to share the words they have made with classmates because hearing and using new words is an important part of learning them.

Read and Reason

7. Distribute the *Read and Reason: Negative Prefix in-* activity sheets (pages 46–47) to students. Have students read one or both passages and answer the comprehension questions on a separate sheet of paper. Ask students to circle the *in-* words they find. If the passages are too difficult for independent reading, ask students to read in pairs or follow along as you read aloud. If you read the passage to them, tell them to raise their hands when they hear an *in-* word. After they (or you) have finished reading, discuss the passage. Ask student volunteers to identify *in-* words and explain what they mean.

Extend and Explore

Choose from among the activities located in Appendix B to give students extra practice with *in-* words.

Answer Key

Divide and Conquer: Negative Prefix *in-* (page 44)

Students' answers for the "definition" section may vary; accept a range of answers.

1. incorrect: not; correct; not correct
2. inflexible: not; flexible; not flexible
3. incomplete: not; complete; not complete
4. inactive: not; active; not active
5. invisible: not; visible; not visible
6. inexpensive: not; expensive; not expensive

Combine and Create: Negative Prefix *in-* (page 45)

1. incorrect
2. incomplete
3. inactive
4. inexpensive
5. inedible

Students' pictures will vary.

Read and Reason: Negative Prefix *in-* (pages 46–47)

Passage A: *incomplete, incorrect, inactive*

Students' answers will vary.

Passage B: *inedible, independently, inactive, incorrect, inexpensive, incomplete*

Students' answers will vary.

Name: _____   Date: _____

Divide and Conquer:
Negative Prefix *in-*

Directions: Break apart each word. Write the prefix and its meaning, the base word, and a simple definition for each word. An example has been done for you.

word	prefix means	base word	definition
❶ incorrect	*in-* = not	correct	not correct
❷ inflexible			
❸ incomplete			
❹ inactive			
❺ invisible			
❻ inexpensive			

Name: _____   Date: _____

Combine and Create:
Negative Prefix *in-*

Directions: When *in-* is added to a base word, it changes the meaning of the base. Sometimes *in-* can even turn a base into its opposite! Add *in-* to the bases to find their opposites. Draw a picture of each new *in-* word.

word	opposite	picture
❶ correct		
❷ complete		
❸ active		
❹ expensive		
❺ edible		

Name: _____   Date: _____

Read and Reason:
Negative Prefix *in-*

Directions: Read the passage. Circle the words with the negative prefix *in-*. Then, complete the activity on a separate sheet of paper by following the instructions.

Passage A

Mother Goose

These are incomplete. Complete them.

The itsy bitsy spider climbed up the _____.
Down came the _____ and washed the spider _____.

Jack be nimble, Jack be _____.
Jack _____ over the candle _____.

These are incorrect. Correct them.

Mack and Jill went down the hill
To dump a pail of soapsuds.

Little Boy Blue, come play your drum.
The sheep's in the meadow, the cow's chewing gum.

Are these active or inactive? Tell why.

Once I saw a little bird
Come hop, hop, hop.

Little Poll Parrot
Sat in his garret
Eating toast and tea.

Name: _____   Date: _____

Read and Reason:
Negative Prefix *in-* (cont.)

Directions: Read the passage. Circle the words with the negative prefix *in-*. Then, answer the questions.

Passage B

Growing a Garden

I want to grow a garden. I want to plant tomatoes, beans, and cucumbers. I also want to plant some inedible things—flowers! And I want to do this all by myself. My dad offered to help, but I said, "No. I want to do this independently."

First, I looked around our whole yard to find a good spot for the garden. I wanted an inactive place. I did not want to put the garden where my brother and sister play. I found a spot but decided it was incorrect. That spot did not get enough sun. I found another spot that was perfect. It gets sun, and it's out of the way of backyard games.

Next, my mom and I went to the garden store. I had to decide— did I want seeds or small plants for my garden? I decided to buy seeds because they were inexpensive.

Now, I have planted my seeds. I have been watering my garden. But my project is still incomplete. It will be complete when the vegetables can be eaten and when the flowers bloom. I can't wait!

Did the author of the passage think of everything for the garden?
Why or why not?

Negative Prefixes *im-* and *il-*

> **Standards:** Uses a variety of sentence structures to expand and embed ideas (McREL 2.3)
> Uses conventions of spelling in written compositions (McREL 3.7)
> Uses phonetic and structural analysis techniques, syntactic structure, and semantic context to decode unknown words (McREL 5.4)

Materials

- *Divide and Conquer: Negative Prefixes im- and il-* (page 50)

- *Combine and Create: Negative Prefixes im- and il-* (page 51)

- *Read and Reason: Negative Prefixes im- and il-* (pages 52–53)

Teaching Tips

- This lesson focuses on negative prefixes *im-* and *il-*, which, like *in-*, negate a word (e.g., *impossible*, meaning "not" "possible"; *illegal*, meaning "not" "legal").

- Reminder: Like the prefix *in-*, the prefixes *im-* and *il-* may also be directional, meaning "in, on, into" (e.g., *import*, meaning to "carry" "into" an area; *illuminate*, meaning to shed "light" "on" something). The prefixes *im-* and *il-* are assimilated forms of the prefix *in-*, which was presented in the previous lesson. (For more on assimilation, see pages 6–8.)

Guided Practice · · · · · · · · · · · · ·

Activate Background Knowledge

1. Write the word *movable* on the board. Have students generate a list of objects that are *movable*. Then, add the prefix *im-* to the word *movable*. Have students generate a list of objects that are immovable, or not movable. Point out how adding the prefix *im-* changes the meaning to mean "not" movable. Tell students that *im-* is a prefix that means "not." Have students generate other *im-* words and explain their meaning, using "not" (e.g., If you are *impatient*, you are "not" patient).

2. Repeat this process with the word *legal*. Have students generate a list of words that represent activities that are legal. Then, add the prefix *il-* to *legal*. Have students generate a list of activities that are illegal, or not legal. Again, point out how adding the prefix *il-* changes the meaning of the word. Tell students that *il-* is a prefix that means "not." Have students generate other *il-* words and explain their meaning, using "not" (e.g., If an argument is *illogical*, it is "not" logical).

3. Tell students that like the prefix *in-*, prefixes *im-* and *il-* change words from positive to negative. In fact, they are just variations of the negative prefix *in-* for pronunciation purposes. Ask students to say *impossible* and then to say *inpossible*. Which is easier to pronounce? Ask them to say *illegible* and then *inlegible*. Again, which is easier to pronounce? Explain that sometimes prefixes change spelling to make pronunciation easier. Share with students that this process is called *assimilation*.

Negative Prefixes *im-* and *il-* (cont.)

Divide and Conquer

4. Distribute the *Divide and Conquer: Negative Prefixes im- and il-* activity sheet (page 50) to students. Guide students through the activity sheet. Quickly point out that in all the words beginning with *im-*, the next letter in each word is either a "p" or an "m"; for each word beginning with *il-*, the next letter in each word is a second "l." As each word is completed, ask students to share and explain their definitions. Make sure students use "not" in their definitions.

Combine and Create

5. Distribute the *Combine and Create: Negative Prefixes im- and il-* activity sheet (page 51) to students. Ask students to work in pairs to sort base words into two categories: those that combine with *im-* and those that combine with *il-*. Have students talk in pairs or as a whole class about how they sorted the words. Have students draw pictures to visually represent the *im-* and *il-* words they find most interesting. Then, have students swap drawings to figure out what words their partners have drawn.

Read and Reason

6. Distribute the *Read and Reason: Negative Prefixes im- and il-* activity sheets (pages 52–53) to students. Have students read one or both passages and answer the comprehension questions on a separate sheet of paper. Ask students to circle the *im-* and *il-* words they find. If the passages are too difficult for independent reading, ask students to read in pairs or follow along as you read aloud. If you read the passage to them, tell them to raise their hands when they hear an *im-* or *il-* word. After they (or you) have finished reading, discuss the passage. Ask student volunteers to identify *im-* and *il-* words and explain their meanings.

Extend and Explore

Choose from among the activities located in Appendix B to give students extra practice with negative *im-* and *il-* words.

Answer Key

Divide and Conquer: Negative Prefixes *im-* and *il-* (page 50)

Students' answers for the "definition" section may vary; accept a range of answers.

1. impolite: not; polite; not polite
2. impatient: not; patient; not patient
3. illegal: not; legal; not legal
4. imperfect: not; perfect; not perfect
5. impossible: not; possible; not possible
6. illiterate: not; literate; not able to read or write

Combine and Create: Negative Prefixes *im-* and *il-* (page 51)

Makes a word with *im-*: *possible, mature, mobile, movable, proper, patient, pure*

Makes a word with *il-*: *legal, literate, logical*

Two synonyms: *immobile* and *immovable*

Students' drawings will vary.

Read and Reason: Negative Prefixes *im-* and *il-* (pages 52–53)

Passage A: *impolite, imperfectly, impossible, improbable, impatient*

Students' answers will vary.

Passage B: *impatient, illegal, impolite, improbable, immature, illogical, Improper*

Students' answers will vary.

Name: _____ Date: _____

Divide and Conquer:
Negative Prefixes *im-* and *il-*

Directions: Break apart each word. Write the prefix and its meaning, the base word, and a simple definition for each word. An example has been done for you.

word	prefix means	base word	definition
❶ impolite	*im-* = not	polite	not polite
❷ impatient			
❸ illegal			
❹ imperfect			
❺ impossible			
❻ illiterate			

Name: _____   Date: _____

Combine and Create:
Negative Prefixes *im-* and *il-*

Directions: Sort the base words under the prefix that matches. Then, complete the activity sheet.

| legal | possible | mature | literate | mobile |
| movable | patient | proper | logical | pure |

Makes a word with *im-*	**Makes a word with *il-***

Which two words that you sorted are synonyms?

_____   _____

Which word do you like best? Draw a picture to show its meaning. Then, trade your drawing with a partner. Can he or she figure out your word?

Name: _____   Date: _____

Read and Reason:
Negative Prefixes *im*- and *il*-

Directions: Read the passage. Circle the words with the negative prefixes *im*- and *il*-. Then, answer the question.

Passage A

Impossible? Depends on Your Genes

I know a boy who can touch the tip of his nose with his tongue. His mother thinks this is impolite. I think it's pretty amazing! Fewer than one percent of people can do this, even imperfectly.

Here are a few more (almost) impossible things to do with your body:

- Raise one eyebrow

- Lick your elbow

- Twitch your nose back and forth

- Wiggle your ears

- Using your right hand and leg, write the number six while making clockwise circles with your leg or vice versa if you are left-handed

These seem strange, don't they? The first four on the list, like touching your nose with your tongue, are genetic. A few people can do them, but most cannot. It's improbable that you can do any of them, but try!

You can teach yourself to write the number six with your right hand while making clockwise circles with your leg. But don't be impatient! It will take practice.

Can you do any of these things? Write about what happened.

Name: _____   Date: _____

Read and Reason:
Negative Prefixes *im-* and *il-* (cont.)

Directions: Read the passage. Circle the words with the negative prefixes *im-* and *il-*. Then, answer the question.

Passage B

Illegal and Strange!

My family likes to collect strange facts. It's like a hobby for us. Last week, my dad found a website that lists laws that are certainly strange! Here are some of our favorites:

- Don't be impatient to get to places in Indiana. It's illegal to ride a horse at speeds greater than 10 miles per hour.

- It's impolite to serve wine in teacups. In Kansas, it's also illegal.

- It's illegal to take a lion to the movies in Maryland. Incredible!

- This one is improbable. It's illegal to let a donkey sleep in the bathtub in Oklahoma. It doesn't matter if the donkey is mature or immature. It's still illegal!

- Restaurants in Wisconsin must serve butter. Customers who want margarine must request it.

What do you think? Are these laws illogical? Improper? Perhaps. They certainly are strange!

> Which law is your favorite? Tell why you think it became a law.

Negative Prefix *dis-*

Standards: Uses a variety of sentence structures to expand and embed ideas (McREL 2.3)
Uses conventions of spelling in written compositions (McREL 3.7)
Uses phonetic and structural analysis techniques, syntactic structure, and semantic context to decode unknown words (McREL 5.4)

Materials

- *Divide and Conquer: Negative Prefix dis-* (page 56)

- *Combine and Create: Negative Prefix dis-* (page 57)

- *Read and Reason: Negative Prefix dis-* (pages 58–59)

Teaching Tips

- This lesson presents the prefix *dis-*, which means "not." In more advanced vocabulary, *dis-* can also mean "apart" or "in different directions."

- When the prefix *dis-* attaches to whole words, it often means "not" (e.g., *dishonest, disable*), although it can also mean "not" when it attaches to some bases (e.g., *disgust, disdain*).

Guided Practice

Activate Background Knowledge

1. Begin the lesson by surveying the class. Ask students to raise their hands if they like to play basketball (or eat broccoli, watch scary movies, etc.—any topic that students will likely have diverse opinions about). Tally the number of students who like basketball. Write this on the board. Next, ask students to raise their hands if they dislike basketball. Tally this number and write it on the board. Point out that students who *dislike* basketball do "not" "like" it. Then, state that members of the class *disagree* because they do "not" "agree" about the topic.

2. Ask students to generate additional *dis-* words they may know. Use the following prompts if students need help:

   - Christina's mother told her to button her coat. When Christina got outside, she unbuttoned her coat. Christina _____ her mother. (*disobeyed*)

   - The magician made the dove vanish into thin air, as if it had never appeared. The dove _____. (*disappeared*)

Divide and Conquer

3. Distribute the *Divide and Conquer: Negative Prefix dis-* activity sheet (page 56) to students. Guide students through the activity sheet. Note that most of the words in this Divide and Conquer contain full bases.

Negative Prefix *dis-* *(cont.)*

Combine and Create

4. Distribute the *Combine and Create: Negative Prefix dis-* activity sheet (page 57) to students. This Combine and Create has two parts. The first part contains more familiar vocabulary and words with intact bases. Have students work with partners to complete cloze sentences. The second part contains more abstract vocabulary and bases that do not stand alone as full words. Have students work with partners to match the words with the corresponding pictures. Having students work in pairs is important because it offers them the opportunity to talk about the new vocabulary they are studying. Talking about words is an effective means of learning them, particularly if the vocabulary deals with abstract concepts.

Read and Reason

5. Distribute the *Read and Reason: Negative Prefix dis-* activity sheets (pages 58–59) to students. Have students read one or both passages and answer the comprehension questions on a separate sheet of paper. Ask students to circle the *dis-* words they find. If the passages are too difficult for independent reading, ask students to read in pairs or follow along as you read aloud. If you read the passage to them, tell them to raise their hands when they hear a *dis-* word. After they (or you) have finished reading, discuss the passage. Ask student volunteers to identify *dis-* words and explain what they mean.

> ### Extend and Explore
>
> Choose from among the activities located in Appendix B to give students extra practice with the prefix *dis-*.

Answer Key

Divide and Conquer: Negative Prefix *dis-* (page 56)

Students' answers for the "definition" section may vary; accept a range of answers.

1. disobey: not; obey; to not obey
2. dislike: not; like; to not like
3. dishonest: not; honest; not honest
4. disagree: not; agree; to not agree
5. disappear: not; appear; to not appear, not able to be seen
6. disregard: not; regard; to give no regard or heed to

Combine and Create: Negative Prefix *dis-* (page 57)

1. disobey
2. dislike
3. dishonest
4. disrespect

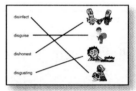

Read and Reason: Negative Prefix *dis-* (pages 58–59)

Passage A: *disuse, disgusting, disposed, disinfecting*

Students' answers will vary.

Passage B: *disposals, disinfects, disposal, disgusting*

Students' answers will vary.

Magic Square (page 60)

1. I
2. D
3. B
4. E
5. C
6. G
7. A
8. H
9. F

Magic Number: 15

Name: _____ Date: _____

Divide and Conquer:
Negative Prefix *dis-*

Directions: Break apart each word. Write the prefix and its meaning, the base word, and a simple definition for each word. An example has been done for you.

word	prefix means	base word	definition
❶ disobey	*dis-* = not	obey	to not obey
❷ dislike			
❸ dishonest			
❹ disagree			
❺ disappear			
❻ disregard			

Name: _____   Date: _____

Combine and Create:
Negative Prefix *dis-*

Directions: Read each sentence. Fill in the blank with the word from the Word Bank that correctly completes each sentence.

Word Bank			
disrespect	dishonest	dislike	disobey

❶ Jeremy went out in the cold without his jacket after his father told him to wear one. Jeremy _____ed his father.

❷ Julia and Scott do not like to eat turnips. They _____ turnips.

❸ Odyssey always tells the truth. If she did not tell the truth, that would be _____.

❹ Tyler bows to his martial arts teacher to show respect. If he did not bow, that would show _____.

Directions: Draw a line matching the picture to the word it shows.

disinfect

disguise

dishonest

disgusting

Name: _____ Date: _____

Read and Reason:
Negative Prefix *dis-*

Directions: Read the passage. Circle the words with the negative prefix *dis-*.
Then, answer the questions.

Passage A

Our Garage Sale

My sister and I wanted to earn some money. We were going to Grandma's house. We wanted to buy souvenirs from her town. Dad suggested that we have a garage sale. We could gather up things that we did not need anymore and sell them to neighborhood kids. What a great idea!

First, we had to find things to sell. We had old toys in what Mom called our "pile of disuse." It was easy to add these to the garage sale. We found a few other things, too.

Next, we had to clean out the garage. It was disgusting! We disposed of trash and swept the floor. We thought about disinfecting everything but decided not to. We set up tables to show our items. We put prices on the items. We just needed customers.

Dad helped us make signs to put around the neighborhood. The signs directed people to our garage. The sale was a success! Now we have money for souvenirs, and some neighborhood kids have new toys.

Do you think a garage sale was the best way for these children to earn money? Why or why not?

Name: _____   Date: _____

Read and Reason:
Negative Prefix *dis-* (cont.)

Directions: Read the passage. Circle the words with the negative prefix *dis-*.
Then, answer the question.

Passage B

Cleaning—the Natural Way

Look around your house in every direction. You will see that keeping things clean is a big job. Some people worry about the harsh chemicals in cleaning products. Vinegar and baking soda, found in most people's kitchens, can clean many different things. These natural cleaning products are safe and natural. They are also inexpensive.

Vinegar and baking soda can be used to clean. Vinegar and water cleans window blinds. Vinegar alone cleans windows, especially when newspaper is used to wipe it off. The vinegar "digests" grease and grime. Soon, the blinds and windows are sparkling.

Together, baking soda and vinegar clean drains and garbage disposals. Vinegar also disinfects. You should stuff a rag in the top of the drain or disposal, though. The vinegar and baking soda will bubble. Directing the bubbles down will make the cleaning faster.

Vinegar gets rid of mildew and even cooking smells! It keeps the diffusion of odors to a minimum. Baking soda and water can clean counters and even the refrigerator. Get rid of the disgusting old food first, though.

Baking soda and vinegar are useful for many different cleaning projects. Best of all, they are natural!

How would you persuade someone to use baking soda and vinegar to clean different things?

Name: _____   Date: _____

Review:
Magic Square

Directions: Match the words with the correct sentences. Then, in the square below, record the number of the question with the correct letter. An example has been done for you. Then, the numbers in each row and column of the square should add up to the Magic Number!

A. ~~unhappy~~   **❶** I'm too _____ to wait for the bus, so I will walk.

B. impolite   **❷** Something _____ is against the law.

C. inactive   **❸** My mother told me it is rude and _____ to stare.

D. illegal   **❹** _____ means "not" "correct."

E. incorrect   **❺** Our sleepy puppy is _____ now.

F. dislike   **❻** _____ pasta is very crunchy.

G. uncooked   **❼** The crying baby is ____unhappy____.

H. dishonest   **❽** Telling a lie is _____.

I. impatient   **❾** Unlike most kids, I _____ chocolate.

A 7	B	C
D	E	F
G	H	I

Magic Number: _____

Prefix *re-*

Standards: Uses a variety of sentence structures to expand and embed ideas (McREL 2.3)
Uses conventions of spelling in written compositions (McREL 3.7)
Uses phonetic and structural analysis techniques, syntactic structure, and semantic context to decode unknown words (McREL 5.4)

Materials

- *Divide and Conquer: Prefix re-* (page 63)

- *Combine and Create: Prefix re-* (page 64)

- *Read and Reason: Prefix re-* (pages 65–66)

Teaching Tips

- *Re-* is the second most common prefix in English, used in over 3,400 words. It can mean either "back" or "again."

- A *prefix* is a unit of meaning that comes at the beginning of a word. It changes the meaning of the word. For example, a library book that is *returned* has been "turned" "back" in. Likewise, a television program that has been *rerun* has been "run" "again."

- A *base* is a unit of meaning that gives the main idea, or basic meaning, of the word.

- The prefix *re-* attaches to both whole words (e.g., *rewrite, redo, recall*) and bases that are not intact words (e.g., *revise, recess, reject*).

Guided Practice ·············

Activate Background Knowledge

1. Review the concept of a prefix (a unit of meaning added to the front of a word that changes the meaning). Tell students that *re-* is a prefix meaning "back" or "again."

2. Discuss with students how in English, we often combine the ideas of "back" and "again." When we *rewrite* a paper, we go "back" and "write it" "again." When we *review* for a test we go "back" and "view" the material "again." This is why many *re-* words include the idea of going back and doing something again.

3. Write the words *turn, read,* and *build* on the board. Point out that adding the prefix *re-* can change each word's meaning. Then, add *re-* to each word. Working with partners or as a whole class, ask students to tell what each *re-* word means. Then, ask students to explain how the prefix changes the meaning (e.g., *return* means to "turn" "back" "again" to a place you have already been). Adding *re-* changes the meaning by adding the direction of "back" or "again."

4. Ask students to brainstorm more *re-* words. Ask them to pick a word from the list, tell what it means, and explain how *re-* changes the meaning of the original word. Where is the idea of "back" or "again" in the word?

5. Point out that since the base provides the meaning of the word, the base comes first when defining the word. For example, *return* means to "turn back," not to "back turn," even though *re-* ("back") comes before "turn."

Prefix *re-* (cont.)

6. Explain that sometimes *re-* joins with a base that is not a complete word (e.g., *recess*). Also explain that sometimes the letter combination "re" is not a prefix (e.g., *read*). Tell students that they can use the meaning to figure out if a word has the prefix *re-*. For example, is there an idea of "back" or "again" in the word *recess*? What about in the word *read*? The discussions students have about these words will reinforce the concept that words are made of units of meaning. It will also help students to develop their word analysis skills.

Divide and Conquer

7. Distribute the *Divide and Conquer: Prefix re-* activity sheet (page 63) to students. Guide students through the activity sheet. As each word is completed, ask a student to explain what it means.

8. Guide students through the first word, *recharge*, by asking, "What is the base?" (charge). "What does the prefix *re-* mean?" ("back" or "again"). "So what does *recharge* mean?" (to "charge" "again"). Repeat this process with the remaining words.

Combine and Create

9. Distribute the *Combine and Create: Prefix re-* activity sheet (page 64) to students. Ask students to work in pairs or independently to sort the bases that make words with the prefix *re-* and bases that do not make words with the prefix *re-*. After sorting the words, ask students to explain how each *re-* word means "back" or "again." With partners, have students choose one *re-* word to act out for the class. Hearing and using words, and even acting them out, are important parts of learning them.

Read and Reason

10. Distribute the *Read and Reason: Prefix re-* activity sheets (pages 65–66) to students. Have students read one or both passages and answer the comprehension questions on a separate sheet of paper. Ask students to circle the *re-* words they find. If the

passages are too difficult for independent reading, ask students to read in pairs or follow along as you read aloud. If you read the passage to them, tell them to raise their hands when they hear a *re-* word. After they (or you) have finished reading, discuss the passage. Ask student volunteers to identify *re-* words and explain their meaning.

Extend and Explore

Choose from among the activities located in Appendix B to give students extra practice with words beginning with the prefix *re-*.

Answer Key

Divide and Conquer: Prefix *re-* (page 63)

Students' answers for the "definition" section may vary; accept a range of answers.

1. recharge: back, again; charge; to charge again
2. rewrite: back, again; write; to write again
3. rerun: back, again; run; to run again
4. rearrange: back, again; arrange; to arrange again
5. rebuild: back, again; build; to build again
6. renew: back, again; new; to make new again

Combine and Create: Prefix *re-* (page 64)

Makes a word with *re-*: *new, fill, cycle, grow, elect, act, fresh, use, pack*

Does not make a word with *re-*: *drive, dance, laugh, jump, sit, walk, joy*

Read and Reason: Prefix *re-* (pages 65–66)

Passage A: *retied, retoasted, repacked, reclosed*

Students' answers will vary.

Passage B: *recycle, Recycling, reuse, recycled, removed, renewed, refreshed, reused, recharged, reusing*

Students' answers will vary.

Name: _____   Date: _____

Divide and Conquer:
Prefix *re-*

Directions: Break apart each word. Write the prefix and its meaning, the base word, and a simple definition for each word. An example has been done for you.

word	prefix means	base word	definition
❶ recharge	*re-* = back, again	charge	to charge again
❷ rewrite			
❸ rerun			
❹ rearrange			
❺ rebuild			
❻ renew			

Name: _____ Date: _____

Combine and Create:
Prefix *re-*

Directions: Some bases make a word with *re-*. Some bases do not make a word with *re-*. Sort these words into the correct columns.

new	fill	cycle	grow	drive	dance	laugh	jump
sit	walk	elect	act	joy	fresh	use	pack

Makes a word with *re-*	Does not make a word with *re-*

Choose one *re-* word to act out for the class. Shh!!! Don't tell your word. Use your actions to help your classmates figure it out!

Name: _____   Date: _____

Read and Reason:
Prefix _re-_

Directions: Read the passage. Circle the words with the directional prefix _re-_.
Then, answer the questions.

Passage A

My Day

I tied my shoes. Then I retied them.

I made some toast. Then I retoasted it.

I packed my backpack. Then I repacked it.

I closed the door. Then I reclosed it.

My name is Pete. Some of my friends call me "Re-Pete"!

Why do you think Pete's friends call him "Re-Pete"?
What do you like to do over and over again?

Name: _____ Date: _____

Read and Reason:
Prefix *re-* (cont.)

Directions: Read the passage. Circle the words with the directional prefix *re-*.
Then, answer the questions.

Passage B

Recycle!

Does your family recycle? In many places, people must recycle. In other places, people choose to recycle. Recycling is important for the environment. So is offering used goods for others to reuse.

Many things can be recycled. Plastic, metal, glass, and paper can be removed and used for other purposes. Even old tires can be recycled. They can be cut up to make soft ground for playgrounds. The tires have a renewed, refreshed purpose.

Materials can also be reused. Many batteries can be recharged. This saves money and also keeps dangerous chemicals out of our trash. Many families support reusing by giving unused clothes or toys to others. Composting is also reusing. Grass clippings and vegetable peels can be turned into rich compost that helps plants grow.

Do you think people should be required to recycle? Why or why not?

Prefix *pre-*

Standards: Uses a variety of sentence structures to expand and embed ideas (McREL 2.3)
Uses conventions of spelling in written compositions (McREL 3.7)
Uses phonetic and structural analysis techniques, syntactic structure, and semantic context to decode unknown words (McREL 5.4)

Materials

- *Divide and Conquer: Prefix pre-* (page 69)

- *Combine and Create: Prefix pre-* (page 70)

- *Read and Reason: Prefix pre-* (pages 71–72)

Teaching Tips

- The directional prefix *pre-* means "before."

- Remind students that prefixes can attach to both whole words and bases.

- The prefix *pre-* attaches to both whole words (e.g., *preheat*, *preview*) and to bases that are not intact words (e.g., *predict*, *prepare*). A *base* is a unit of meaning that gives the main idea, or basic meaning, of the word.

- The focus of this lesson is primarily on words in which *pre-* attaches to whole words. The words *predict* and *prefix*, however, attach to Latin bases. They have been included because they occur frequently in academic vocabulary and students will likely have prior knowledge of them.

Guided Practice · · · · · · · · · · · ·

Activate Background Knowledge

1. Write the word *preview* on the board. Ask students if they have ever seen a *preview* at the movies. Ask them if the preview was shown before or after the movie. Give them time to answer. Explain that *pre-* is a prefix that means "before" as in the word *preview* (an advertisement for a movie that is "viewed" "before" a movie). Put a slash between the prefix *pre-* and the base word *view* to help students see how the word is built.

2. Now write the word *predict* on the board. Put a slash between *pre-* and *dict*. Tell students that *dict* is a Latin base that means "to say" or "to tell." Ask students to explain what it means to *predict* the outcome of a book or movie (they "tell" the ending "before" it happens).

3. Working with partners, ask students to brainstorm more *pre-* words. Then, ask each pair to pick a word from the list, tell what it means, and explain how adding the prefix *pre-* changes the meaning. Use the following sentences if students need help:

   - The cookie recipe said to heat the oven before putting the cookies in. _____ing the oven warms it up so the dough will rise. (*Preheat*)

   - The dishes were so dirty that I had to soak them before I could wash them. I had to _____ the dishes. (*presoak*)

   - I dislike washing salad leaves, so I always buy bags of salad that are washed before I buy them. I buy _____ salad. (*prewashed*)

Prefix *pre-* *(cont.)*

Divide and Conquer

4. Distribute the *Divide and Conquer: Prefix pre-* activity sheet (page 69) to students. Guide students through the activity sheet. As each word is completed, ask students to explain its meanings. Make sure their definitions are accurate.

Combine and Create

5. Distribute the *Combine and Create: Prefix pre-* activity sheet (page 70) to students. Ask students to work in pairs or independently as they consider these *pre-* words in context. At the end of the exercise, invite students to share their answers and explain why they chose each word. Ask them to explain how each *pre-* word means "before." Hearing, using, and even talking about new words are important parts of learning them.

Read and Reason

6. Distribute the *Read and Reason: Prefix pre-* activity sheets (pages 71–72) to students. Have students read one or both passages and answer the comprehension questions on a separate sheet of paper. Ask students to circle the *pre-* words they find. If the passages are too difficult for independent reading, ask students to read in pairs or follow along as you read aloud. If you read the passage to them, tell them to raise their hands when they hear a *pre-* word. After they (or you) have finished reading, discuss the passage. Ask student volunteers to identify *pre-* words and explain what they mean.

Extend and Explore

Choose from among the activities located in Appendix B to give students extra practice with words beginning with the prefix *pre-*.

Answer Key

Divide and Conquer: Prefix *pre-* (page 69)

Students' answers for the "definition" section may vary; accept a range of answers.

1. prepay: before; pay; pay before
2. preview: before; view; view before
3. premix: before; mix; mix before
4. preheat: before; heat; heat before
5. predict: before; say, tell; say, tell before
6. presoak: before; soak; soak before

Combine and Create: Prefix *pre-* (page 70)

1. preheat
2. predict
3. premixed
4. prejudge
5. prehistoric
6. prepackaged
7–8. Students' sentences will vary; ensure that the sentences make sense and demonstrate an understanding of the concepts taught.

Read and Reason: Prefix *pre-* (pages 71–72)

Passage A: *preview, Prebaked, prebaked, Precooked, precooked, Presliced, presliced*

Students' answers will vary.

Passage B: *prefabricated, prepared, premixed, prepacked, preplaced, preheated, precautions, predates*

Students' answers will vary.

Name: _____   Date: _____

Divide and Conquer:
Prefix *pre-*

Directions: Break apart each word. Write the prefix and its meaning, the base word, and a simple definition for each word. An example has been done for you.

word	prefix means	base word	definition
1 prepay	*pre-* = before	pay	pay before
2 preview			
3 premix			
4 preheat			
5 predict		*dict* = say, tell	
6 presoak			

Name: _____ Date: _____

Combine and Create:
Prefix *pre-*

Directions: Using the Word Bank, fill in the blanks with words that start with *pre-*.

Word Bank		
preheat	prepackaged	prejudge
predict	prehistoric	premixed

❶ The recipe said to _____ the oven to 350 degrees. That way, the oven will warm up before you put the food in it.

❷ I like to _____ the events in a book before I read it.

❸ Ingredients for the ready-bake cake were _____. I didn't have to mix them at all!

❹ Don't _____ a book before you read it!

❺ Dinosaurs lived on Earth in _____ times.

❻ When Christina bought her mother's birthday present, it already came in a pretty package. It was _____.

Directions: Write your own sentences using the words.

❼ Prepay: _____

_____

_____

❽ Precook: _____

_____

_____

Name: _____   Date: _____

Read and Reason:
Prefix *pre-*

Directions: Read the passage. Circle the words with the directional prefix *pre-*.
Then, answer the questions.

Passage A

Preview of My Dinner

Here is a preview of my dinner. I don't know why, but I was
thinking about "Three Blind Mice." Strange, right?

Prebaked bread. Prebaked bread.
Soft and warm. Soft and warm.
Oatmeal or wheat, what a treat!
I prefer mine with some turkey meat.
Without it my lunch would be incomplete,
Prebaked bread.

Precooked peas. Precooked peas.
Sweet and green. Sweet and green.
Mother has told me all of my life,
"Never eat peas without your knife!"
Did you ever try such a task in your life?
Precooked peas.

Presliced meat. Presliced meat.
Warmed in the oven. Warmed in the oven.
Salome, chicken, turkey, or beef,
All of these meats sliced thin as a leaf.
Thinking about them makes me want to eat.
Presliced meat.

Is this a healthy meal? Why or why not?

Name: _____ Date: _____

Read and Reason:
Prefix *pre-* (cont.)

Directions: Read the passage. Circle the words with the directional prefix *pre-*. Then, answer the questions.

Passage B

Prefabricated Homes

As you know, *pre-* means "before." *Fabricated* means "made" or "constructed." From this, can you figure out what a "prefabricated home" is? It is a home that is made somewhere else. Then, the pieces are brought to the home site and put together.

How does all this happen? Materials are prepared. Paint is premixed. Walls and floors are made and then prepacked for travel. Windows are preplaced in walls. Even electricity is checked, and the furnace and oven are preheated to make sure they work. The prefabricated house builders take all these precautions so that the new house will be easy and safe to put together.

You have probably seen prefabricated homes. Since the 1950s, they have been inexpensive housing for many people. But their use predates the 1950s. To begin with, prefabricated homes were meant to be mobile, so they could move with people as they went to another city. This is why they are sometimes called "mobile homes." Today's prefabricated homes are usually stationary, or immobile.

Do you think prefabricated homes are a good idea? Why or why not?

Prefix *ex-*

Standards: Uses a variety of sentence structures to expand and embed ideas (McREL 2.3)
Uses conventions of spelling in written compositions (McREL 3.7)
Uses phonetic and structural analysis techniques, syntactic structure, and semantic context to decode unknown words (McREL 5.4)

Materials

- *Divide and Conquer: Prefix ex-* (page 75)

- *Combine and Create: Prefix ex-* (page 76)

- *Read and Reason: Prefix ex-* (pages 77–78)

Teaching Tips

- The prefix *ex-* means "out."

- *Ex-* can attach to both whole words and Latin bases. When the prefix *ex-* is hyphenated and attached to a whole word, it usually means "former, no longer" (*ex-employer*). This lesson focuses on non-hyphenated words in which *ex-* means "out."

- Because *ex-* frequently attaches to Latin bases, this lesson focuses on familiar academic words in which *ex-* attaches to bases (e.g., *exclaim*, *expel*). The meanings of the Latin bases are provided. The objective is for students to internalize the meaning of the prefix *ex-* while working with words that deal with familiar concepts. This is a good opportunity to emphasize that prefixes often attach to bases as well as to whole words.

Guided Practice · · · · · · · · · · · ·

Activate Background Knowledge

1. Review the concept of a prefix (a unit added to the front of a word that influences its meaning). Write the word *exit* on the board. Ask a student to *exit* the room and then come back. Ask the class where the student went when he or she *exited* the room. Draw their attention to the idea that he or she went "out" of the room. Tell students that *ex-* is a prefix meaning "out."

2. Next, write the word *exhale* on the board. Ask students to exhale. Where did their breath go when they exhaled? (It went out of their bodies.) Put a slash between *ex-* and *hale*. Explain that *hale* is a Latin base that means "breathe." Remind students that the base (*hale*) carries the main meaning, so *exhale* means to "breathe" "out."

3. Have students work with partners to generate other *ex-* words they may know. Use the following sentences if students need help:

- When I got an A on my report card, I was so excited that I shouted out in joy! I _____, "I got an A!" (*exclaimed*)

- When the volcano erupted, lava _____ everywhere! (*exploded*)

- In P.E., we stretch our muscles by _____ing our arms and legs. (*extend*)

Prefix ex- *(cont.)*

Divide and Conquer

4. Distribute the *Divide and Conquer: Prefix ex-* activity sheet (page 75) to students. Guide students through the activity sheet. In this Divide and Conquer, *ex-* attaches to Latin bases. The concepts of many of these words may be familiar to students (e.g., *explode*, *exhale*). The meanings of the bases is provided. As students work, ensure that they explain where the meaning of "out" is in the words. For example, in the word *explode*, matter "bursts" "out" of an object.

Combine and Create

5. Distribute the *Combine and Create: Prefix ex-* activity sheet (page 76) to students. First, students match each *ex-* word with its counterpart. Then, students match *ex-* words with their opposites. (Note that the pictures serve to illustrate the abstract concepts.) At the end of the exercise, ask students to share their answers because talking about and hearing new words are important parts of learning them. Encourage students to use the word *out* as they talk about *ex-* words.

Read and Reason

6. Distribute the *Read and Reason: Prefix ex-* activity sheets (pages 77–78) to students. Have students read one or both passages and answer the comprehension questions on a separate sheet of paper. Ask students to circle the *ex-* words they find. If the passages are too difficult for independent reading, ask students to read in pairs or follow along as you read aloud. If you read the passage to them, tell them to raise their hands when they hear an *ex-* word. After they (or you) have finished reading, discuss the passage. Ask student volunteers to identify *ex-* words and explain their meaning.

Extend and Explore

Choose from among the activities located in Appendix B to give students extra practice with words beginning with the prefix *ex-*.

Answer Key

Divide and Conquer: Prefix *ex-* (page 75)

Students' answers for the "definition" section may vary; accept a range of answers.

1. exit: out; go; go out
2. exclaim: out; shout; shout out
3. explode: out; burst; burst out
4. exhale: out; breathe; breathe out
5. exclude: out; shut, close; shut out
6. expel: out; push; push out

Combine and Create: Prefix *ex-* (page 76)

Part 1:

1. C	4. B
2. A	5. E
3. D	6. F

Part 2:

exit—enter

exhale—inhale

exclaim—quiet

exclude—include

Read and Reason: Prefix *ex-* (pages 77–78)

Passage A: *ex, Exes, extend, exhale, excursions, exclaim, expel, explosives, ex-friends, exciting*

Students' answers will vary.

Passage B: *expand, exporting, exporter, exports, Exporting, exportation, export, expense, extend*

Students' answers will vary.

Name: _____   Date: _____

Divide and Conquer:
Prefix ex-

Directions: Break apart each word. Write the prefix and its meaning and a simple definition for each word. An example has been done for you.

word	prefix means	base word	definition
❶ exit	ex- = out	*it*- = go	go out
❷ exclaim		*claim*- = shout	
❸ explode		*plode* = burst	
❹ exhale		*hale* = breathe	
❺ exclude		*clud* = shut, close	
❻ expel		*pel* = push	

Name: _____   Date: _____

Combine and Create:
Prefix ex-

Directions: Each word contains the prefix *ex-* and each statement contains the word "out." Match each word with the right statement.

❶ extinguish

❷ explode

❸ exclaim

❹ extend

❺ exhale

❻ expire

A. I am what happens when you put too much air in a balloon and it bursts out.

B. I am what you do when you stretch out your arms and legs after a nap.

C. I am what you do to put out a fire.

D. I am what you do when you are so excited you just have to shout out!

E. I am what you do when you let out a big breath of relief.

F. I am what happens when food is old. Don't eat me! Throw me out!

Directions: Draw a line to match each picture and *ex-* word with its opposite.

exit

exhale

exclaim

exclude

quiet

include

inhale

enter

Name: _____   Date: _____

Read and Reason:
Prefix *ex-*

Directions: Read the passage. Circle the words with the directional prefix *ex-*. Then, answer the question.

Passage A

The Exes

Lexie is my best friend. She's always saying that she hates her name. "No one else has *ex* in their name," she says.

So my friends and I started a club. We decided to give ourselves secret club names that had *ex*. We used the first letter of our names and then added *ex*. So Josie is now Jex. Rick is Rex. And Tony is Tex. Tina is Tex, too, so she is Tex 2! And of course, we have Lexie. We call ourselves *The Exes*.

We try to do *ex* things at our club meetings. We extend hands to each other. We even exhale at the same time. We take excursions through the neighborhood. And we exclaim, "We love *ex*!"

The Exes

We do not do some *ex* things. We do not expel each other. We do not touch explosives. We are not ex-friends.

We think our *ex* club is exciting. And Lexie likes it because now we all have *ex* in our names!

How do The Exes show friendship?

Name: _____   Date: _____

Read and Reason:
Prefix ex (cont.)

Directions: Read the passage. Circle the words with the directional prefix *ex-*. Then, answer the question.

Passage B

Exports

Companies that make things want to sell the things they make. This is how they make profits. This is also how their businesses expand, or grow. If they sell their products in another country, this is called *exporting*. An exporter is a company or person that exports products. Those from other countries who buy these products are importers. Exporting and importing are major parts of international trade.

The United States has some rules for exportation. The company needs a license to export. It is illegal to export to some countries. Currently, companies in the United States cannot export to North Korea or Iran. Tariffs (taxes) may be added to the expense of the products.

In spite of these limits, many companies export products to other countries. They see this as a good way to extend the growth of their companies.

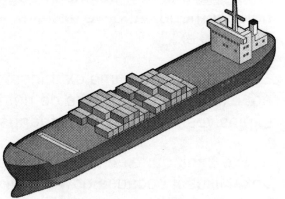

In the United States, airplanes, cars, and food are the three largest exports. Why do you think this is so?

Prefix *sub-*

Standards: Uses a variety of sentence structures to expand and embed ideas (McREL 2.3)
Uses conventions of spelling in written compositions (McREL 3.7)
Uses phonetic and structural analysis techniques, syntactic structure, and semantic context to decode unknown words (McREL 5.4)

Materials

- *Divide and Conquer: Prefix sub-* (page 81)
- *Combine and Create: Prefix sub-* (page 82)
- *Read and Reason: Prefix sub-* (pages 83–84)

Teaching Tips

- *Sub-* means "under" or "below."

- Because *sub-* attaches to whole words and Latin bases, this lesson is a good opportunity to remind students that prefixes can attach to both whole words and bases. A *base* is a unit of meaning that gives the main idea, or basic meaning, of the word. It can be a whole word (sub*zero*) or a word part (sub*tract*). In this lesson, familiar *sub-* words attach to bases (*subtract, substitute, submerge*). Base meanings are provided for students.

Guided Practice · · · · · · · · · · · · ·

Activate Background Knowledge

1. Review the concept of a prefix (a unit added to the front of a word that changes its meaning). Write the word *submarine* on the board. Ask students where a submarine travels. Point out that a submarine travels "under" water. Tell students that marine means "sea," so a *submarine* literally travels "under" the "sea." Explain that *sub-* is a prefix meaning "under" or "below." Put a slash between *sub-* and *marine* to draw students' attention to how the word is built.

2. Repeat this process with the word *subway*. Write *subway* on the board. Ask students where a subway travels. Point out that the subway is a *way* to travel that is "under" ground. Put a slash between *sub-* and *way* to draw students' attention to how the word is built.

3. Ask students to generate other *sub-* words they may know. As they come up with words, ask them to explain how the words demonstrate the concept of "under."

4. If students need assistance generating words, use the following sentences as prompts:

   - When the temperature drops below zero, it is too cold to go outside. It is _____. (*subzero*)

   - To find the difference in a math problem, you put the smaller number under the greater number and _____. (*subtract*)

   - Earthquakes occur when plates below the Earth's surface shift. These plates are _____. (*subterranean*)

Prefix *sub-* (cont.)

Divide and Conquer

5. Distribute the *Divide and Conquer: Prefix sub-* activity sheet (page 81) to students. Guide students through the activity sheet. In this Divide and Conquer, students will encounter words with bases that are intact words as well as words that contain Latin bases. Latin bases have been provided for students.

Combine and Create

6. Distribute the *Combine and Create: Prefix sub-* activity sheet (page 82) to students. Using the Word Bank, ask students to work in pairs to write each completed *sub-* word in the blank that best fits the described situation. At the end of the exercise, ask students to share their responses with the class. Make sure to explain how each *sub-*word means "under" or "below." Hearing, using, and even talking about new words are important parts of learning them.

7. Then, have students draw pictures to illustrate *sub-* words that deal with abstract concepts. Drawing helps students visualize abstract concepts, thereby supporting their understanding of higher-level vocabulary.

Read and Reason

8. Distribute the *Read and Reason: Prefix sub-* activity sheets (pages 83–84) to students. Have students read one or both passages and answer the comprehension questions on a separate sheet of paper. Ask students to circle the *sub-* words they find. If the passages are too difficult for independent reading, ask students to read in pairs or follow along as you read aloud. If you read the passage to them, tell them to raise their hands when they hear a *sub-* word. After they (or you) have finished reading, discuss the passage. Ask student volunteers to identify *sub-* words and explain their meaning.

> ## Extend and Explore
> Choose from among the activities located in Appendix B to give students extra practice with words with the prefix *sub-*.

Answer Key

Divide and Conquer: Prefix *sub-* (page 81)

Students' answers for the "definition" section may vary; accept a range of answers.

1. subtitle: under, below; title; a title below the main title; also text printed under the images on a television or movie screen
2. submerge: under, below; plunge; plunge under
3. subtract: under, below; pull, draw, drag; to reduce by drawing a lower number "out from under" a higher number
4. subzero: under, below; zero; below zero
5. subhuman: under, below; human; less than human
6. subterranean: under, below; earth; below the Earth's surface

Combine and Create: Prefix *sub-* (page 82)

Part1:

1. subway
2. subzero
3. subtract
4. subterranean
5. submarine
6. subplot

Part 2:

Students' drawings will vary.

Read and Reason: Prefix *sub-* (pages 83–84)

Passage A: *sub-, subtracting, subdivide, subway, subfloor*

Students' answers will vary.

Passage B: *subway, Subways, subterranean, subdivided, suburbs*

Students' answers will vary.

Name: _____   Date: _____

Divide and Conquer:
Prefix *sub-*

Directions: Break apart each word. Write the prefix and its meaning, the base word, and a simple definition for each word. An example has been done for you.

word	prefix means	base word	definition
❶ subtitle	*sub-* = under, below	title	a title below the main title
❷ submerge		*merg-* = plunge, dip	
❸ subtract		*tract-* = pull, draw, drag	
❹ subzero			
❺ subhuman			
❻ subterranean		*terra-* = land, Earth	

Name: _____   Date: _____

Combine and Create:
Prefix *sub-*

Directions: Write the *sub-* word from the Word Bank below that best fits the described situation.

Word Bank		
subplot	subzero	submarine
subway	subtract	subterranean

❶ New York City has an elaborate underground train system so people can get around without cars. _____

❷ During the blizzard, the temperature outside dropped below zero.
_____

❸ "Four minus two equals two." _____

❹ The inner core of the Earth is under its surface. _____

❺ In the Navy, sailors learn how to drive this underwater vessel.
_____

❻ The book's main plot is about two boys who solve a mystery. There is a smaller plot about a dog that they take in from the street.

_____

Directions: Draw a picture to show what is happening in each sentence.

The temperature was over 100 degrees! The kids were thrilled to *submerge* themselves in the pool.	
I love to read scary stories about zombies and monsters. *Subhuman* creatures are so spooky!	

Name: _____   Date: _____

Read and Reason:
Prefix *sub-*

Directions: Read the passage. Circle the words with the directional prefix *sub-*. Then, answer the questions.

Passage A

Sub- Means Under

In school, we learned that *sub-* means "under." Then, our teacher gave us homework. He said we should list *sub-* words from our weekend. I made little poems instead. Here are a few:

Adding, subtracting, multiplying, too.

I did my math homework. Did you?

At supper, we had to subdivide the pizza pie.

I wanted it all myself. Oh me, oh my!

We took a ride on a subway.

At the end, we found a park for play.

I watched my dad nail down a subfloor.

He didn't hit his finger. What a bore!

Do you think the teacher will like the student's poems?
Why or why not?

Name: _____   Date: _____

Read and Reason:
Prefix *sub-* (cont.)

Directions: Read the passage. Circle the words with the directional prefix *sub-*.
Then, answer the questions.

Passage B

Subways

If you live in or have visited a city, you may have gone on a subway.
Subways are subterranean transportation systems. Have you ever
wondered why people thought it would be a good idea to travel by going
through a tunnel in the earth?

New York City's first subway aimed to solve a problem. The problem
was rapid growth in the early 1800s. New York City's population
increased by almost 60 percent each decade. People suffered on
crowded streets. It seemed to take forever to go just a few blocks.

Publisher Alfred Beach got fed up. He wanted an easier way to
travel. He dug a trench in the streets. Then, rails were laid down.
Finally, supports were set so that the street could be rebuilt. In 1870, he
opened a new way to get around called the "Beach Pneumatic Transit."
This was a subterranean wind tunnel 312 feet long. Twenty-two
passengers sat in a railway car. A big fan pushed the car along tracks.

Today, most big cities have subway systems.
Usually, the city is subdivided. Different rail
lines go to different parts of the city. Many
subway lines also go to the suburbs. Subways
have come a long way since Beach's big fan!

> Have you been on a subway? If so, did you like it? If not, do
> you think you would like it? Why?

Prefix *de-*

Standards: Uses a variety of sentence structures to expand and embed ideas (McREL 2.3)
Uses conventions of spelling in written compositions (McREL 3.7)
Uses phonetic and structural analysis techniques, syntactic structure, and semantic context to decode unknown words (McREL 5.4)

Materials

- *Divide and Conquer: Prefix de-* (page 87)
- *Combine and Create: Prefix de-* (page 88)
- *Read and Reason: Prefix de-* (pages 89–90)

Teaching Tips

- The prefix *de-* means "down." It can also mean "off of." The ideas of "down" and "off of" (i.e., separation) are related: when things come "off" and detach, they tend to fall "down." By contrast, we say that things stay up when they remain attached.

- When *de-* means "down," it can describe a physical downward motion, as in *descending* the stairs. It can also describe the figurative idea of "down," as in feeling *depressed* (feeling *down*).

- When *de-* means "off of," it describes the physical removal of something that has accumulated (e.g., to *defrost* a windshield is to get the frost "off of" it).

- *De-* attaches to both whole words (e.g., *deactivate*, *deplane*) and bases that are not intact words (e.g., *demolish*, *descend*). A *base* is a unit of meaning that gives the main idea of the word. It can be a whole word (*defrost*) or a word part (*demote*). Make sure students talk about how the words represent the ideas of "down" or "off of."

Guided Practice · · · · · · · · · · · · ·

Activate Background Knowledge

1. Show students a picture of a child walking down stairs. Ask students to share what the child is doing. Write the word *descend* on the board. Tell students that the child is walking down—or *descending*—the stairs.

2. Next, show students a picture of people getting off of an airplane. Ask them to identify what is happening in the picture. Write the word *deplane* on the board. Tell students that the passengers are getting off of—or *deplaning*—the aircraft.

3. Ask students what the words *descend* and *deplane* have in common. (*They share the idea of "down" or "off of."*) Ask students to identify the prefix the two words share. Tell students that *de-* is a prefix meaning "down" or "off of." Put a slash between the prefix *de-* and the bases in both words to show students how the words are built.

4. Invite students to generate other *de-* words they may know, paying attention to the idea of "down" and "off of" in the words. If students need assistance, use these sentences as prompts:

   - When my dad starts the car in the morning, the windows are covered in fog. He has to get the fog off the car so he can drive. He _____ the car. (*defogs*)

   - When I took the chicken out of the freezer, it was covered with frost. Before I could cook the chicken, I had to get the frost off, so I left it on the counter to _____. (*defrost*)

Prefix *de-* (cont.)

- There is an old, abandoned, run-down house at the end of my block. So yesterday, a construction company came and tore it down. They _____ed the house. (*demolish*)

Divide and Conquer

5. Distribute the *Divide and Conquer: Prefix de-* activity sheet (page 87) to students. Guide students through the activity sheet. Students will work with words that have both Latin bases and bases that are whole words. The Latin bases have been provided.

Combine and Create

6. Distribute the *Combine and Create: Prefix de-* activity sheet (page 88) to students. Ask students to work individually or in pairs. Upon completion, ask students to read their answers aloud, making sure that they read the definitions that contain the words "down" or "off of."

7. Then, have students write captions to show their understanding of the concepts represented in the pictures. Allow students time to share their captions and discuss how the pictures show the meaning of "down" or "off of."

Read and Reason

8. Distribute the *Read and Reason: Prefix de-* activity sheets (pages 89–90) to students. Have students read one or both passages and answer the comprehension questions on a separate sheet of paper. Ask students to circle the *de-* words they find. If the passages are too difficult for independent reading, ask students to read in pairs or follow along as you read aloud. If you read the passage to them, tell them to raise their hands when they hear a *de-* word. After they (or you) have finished reading, discuss the passage. Ask student volunteers to identify *de-* words and explain their meaning.

Extend and Explore

Choose from among the activities located in Appendix B to give students extra practice with *de-* words.

Answer Key

Divide and Conquer: Prefix *de-* (page 87)

Students' answers for the "definition" section may vary; accept a range of answers.

1. defrost: off of; frost; to remove frost or get frost "off of" an object
2. demolish: down; build; to take down a building or other construction
3. deposit: down; put, place; to put down money into an account (as in "down payment")
4. deflate: down; blow; to let air out or to take the air "down" in an object
5. deplane: off of; plane; to get "off of" an airplane
6. descend: down; climb; to climb "down"

Combine and Create: Prefix *de-* (page 88)

Part 1:

1. E		4. D
2. A		5. B
3. C		

Part 2:

1. defrost		3. depressed
2. deflate		4. deactivate

Students' captions will vary.

Read and Reason: Prefix *de-* (pages 89–90)

Passage A: *dehydrated, deactivated, depressed, degrease, deposits, defrost, deice*

Students' answers will vary.

Passage B: *demolish, depended, depressed, deactivate, deflated*

Students' answers will vary.

Name: _____   Date: _____

Divide and Conquer:
Prefix *de-*

Directions: Break apart each word. Write the prefix and its meaning, the base word, and a simple definition for each word. An example has been done for you.

word	prefix means	base word	definition
❶ defrost	*de-* = off of	frost	to get frost off of
❷ demolish		*mol* = build	
❸ deposit		*posit-* = put, place	
❹ deflate		*flat* = blow	
❺ deplane			
❻ descend		*scend* = climb	

Name: _____   Date: _____

Combine and Create:
Prefix *de-*

Directions: Match each word with the best statement.

❶ dethrone

❷ deactivate

❸ depart

❹ deice

❺ depressed

A. I was racing my remote control car all over the living room until my mother turned the power off.

B. I have been feeling sad and down lately.

C. We must now say goodbye as we part ways.

D. My mom uses a scraper to get the ice off of the car windows in the winter.

E. When the king abused his power, the people forced him to step down from the throne.

Directions: Write a caption for each picture. Include the word the picture is showing. Explain how the picture is showing the idea of "down" or "off of." The first one has been done for you.

Word Bank			
deactivate	depress	deflate	~~defrost~~

❶  **Caption:** The chicken is defrosting. The ice is melting off.

❷  **Caption:** _____

❸ **Caption:** _____

❹ **Caption:** _____

Name: _____   Date: _____

Read and Reason:
Prefix *de-*

Directions: Read the passage. Circle the words with the directional prefix *de-*.
Then, answer the question.

Passage A

Cleaning the Kitchen

Everyone in my family has chores. This week, my chore was to
clean the kitchen. What a mess! Cleaning the microwave and the
refrigerator were the hardest.

The microwave was full of dehydrated bits of food. To clean it, I
first unplugged it. This deactivated the electricity so it was safe to
clean. Then, I depressed the button to open the door. I scrubbed
the sides and plate inside. I had to degrease these surfaces. When
I finished, I closed the door again and plugged the microwave
back in.

The refrigerator was a mess, too.
Strange deposits were on some of the
shelves, so I cleaned them off. I did
not need to defrost the freezer, but I did
need to deice it. Some ice had built up.

Now the whole kitchen looks great!
I hope I don't have to clean it again
next week.

How could grease and dehydrated food get into the microwave?

Name: _____   Date: _____

Read and Reason:
Prefix de- *(cont.)*

Directions: Read the passage. Circle the words with the directional prefix *de-*.
Then, answer the question.

Passage B

My Hot Air Balloon

"Here's your birthday gift from Uncle Mario," said Dad. It was a
big box. I was excited! I looked at the card. It said, "Fly high!" I
wondered what it could be. When I opened the box, I found a model
of a hot air balloon.

First, my dad and I put it together. I was afraid that we would
demolish it before it even had the chance to fly. We depended on
the directions to help us. Finally, it was built. It looked great!

Now the big test—would it fly? We depressed a button to release
air into the balloon. Up it went! It looked beautiful in the sky. After
a few minutes, though, I got worried. "Dad," I said. "How do we get
it down?"

Dad said, "Let's read the directions." So that's
what we did. The first thing to do was to slow down
the airflow into the balloon. We depressed another
button to deactivate the air pump. As the air left
the balloon, it deflated. The whole model air ballon
floated softly back to Earth.

I'm glad it did not crash. I can't wait to "fly high"
again!

> How was reading important for this project?

Prefixes *co-* and *con-*

Standards: Uses a variety of sentence structures to expand and embed ideas (McREL 2.3)
Uses conventions of spelling in written compositions (McREL 3.7)
Uses phonetic and structural analysis techniques, syntactic structure, and semantic context to decode unknown words (McREL 5.4)

Materials

- *Divide and Conquer: Prefixes co- and con-* (page 94)

- *Combine and Create: Prefixes co- and con-* (page 95)

- *Read and Reason: Prefixes co- and con-* (pages 96–97)

Teaching Tips

- *Co-* and *con-* mean "with" or "together."

- *Co-* and *con-* attach to whole words and to bases that are not intact words. In general, *co-* attaches to whole words (e.g., *cooperate, coworker, coauthor*) and *con-* attaches to bases (e.g., *conduct, contract, convene*).

Guided Practice · · · · · · · · · · · ·

Activate Background Knowledge

1. Invite two students to come to the front of the room to act out the concept of *cooperating* with one another. (Students may demonstrate working together, helping each other, etc.) Ask students what they do when they *cooperate* with each other. Draw students' attention to the idea that when they *cooperate*, they work "together."

2. Write the word *cooperate* on the board. Put a slash between the prefix *co-* and the base *operate*. Tell students that *co-* and *con-* are prefixes that mean "with" or "together," so the word *cooperate* literally means "operating" "together."

3. Next, write the words *do* and *not* on the board. Ask students what a writer does when he or she wants to bring two words together, such as *do* and *not*. (He or she turns the words into the contraction *don't*.) Write *don't* underneath *do not*. Ask students what kind of word *don't* is. Invite responses or tell them that *don't* is a contraction. Write *contraction* on the board. Explain that *tract* is a Latin base that means "pull." A contraction literally means a word that is "pulled" "together." Put a slash between *con-* and *traction* to show students how the word is built.

4. Demonstrate this concept again using the words *is, not,* and *isn't*. Ask students to explain how a contraction like *isn't* shows the concept of "with" or "together." (*It is literally the pulling together of two different words.*)

Prefixes *co-* and *con-* (cont.)

5. Ask students to generate other *co-/con-* words they may know. If they need assistance, use the following sentences as prompts:

- The principal and assistant principal work together to run the school. They are _____. (*coworkers*)

- Dogs have learned how to exist peacefully with people; therefore, they make good pets. Dogs and people know how to _____. (*coexist*)

- The musician waved his baton to let the members of the orchestra know when it was time to play their instruments. The musician led the members of the orchestra so they could play together. This musician _____ the orchestra. (*conducted*)

Divide and Conquer

6. Distribute the *Divide and Conquer: Prefixes co- and con-* activity sheet (page 94) to students. Guide students through the activity sheet. You may wish to guide the students through the first word, *construct*, by saying, "If *struct* means 'build' and *con-* means 'with, together,' then *construct* means 'to build something by putting it together.'"

Combine and Create

7. Distribute the *Combine and Create: Prefixes co- and con-* activity sheet (page 95) to students. Ask students to work individually or in pairs. Ask them to add the prefix *co-* or *con-* to the bases listed. Then, ask them to write out the entire *co-* or *con-* word next to the most fitting statement.

Read and Reason

8. Distribute the *Read and Reason: Prefixes co- and con-* activity sheets (pages 96–97) to students. Have students read one or both passages and answer the comprehension questions on a separate sheet of paper. Ask students to circle the *co-* or *con-* words they find. If the passages are too difficult for independent reading, ask students to read in pairs or follow along as you read aloud. If you read the passage to them, tell them to raise their hands when they hear a *co-* or *con-* word. After they (or you) have finished reading, discuss the passage. Ask student volunteers to identify *co-* or *con-* words and explain what they mean.

Extend and Explore

Choose from among the activities located in Appendix B to give students extra practice with words beginning with the prefix *co-* or *con-*.

Prefixes *co-* and *con-* (cont.)

Answer Key

Divide and Conquer: Prefixes *co-* and *con-* (page 94)

Students' answers for the "definition" section may vary; accept a range of answers.

1. construct: with, together; build; to build something by putting it together
2. contraction: with, together; pull, draw, drag; pull together
3. cooperate: with, together; work; to work together
4. coauthor: with, together; author; an author who works together with another author
5. coexist: with, together; exist/live; to exist/ live together
6. copilot: with, together; pilot; a pilot who flies a plane with another pilot

Combine and Create: Prefixes *co-* and *con-* (page 95)

1. coauthor
2. contraction
3. coexist
4. cooperate
5. costar
6. conductor
7. construction

Read and Reason: Prefixes *co-* and *con-* (pages 96–97)

Passage A: *consensus, construct, coillustrated, coauthors, cowritten*

Students' answers will vary.

Passage B: *cooperatives, connect, construction*

Students' answers will vary.

Crossword Puzzle (pages 98–99)

Across:

3. descend
5. subzero
6. cooperate
10. contract
11. coworker
13. submarine

Down:

1. predict
2. defrost
3. deplane
4. exhale
7. exit
8. explode
9. preheat
12. preview
13. subway

Name: _____   Date: _____

Divide and Conquer:

Prefixes *co-* and *con-*

Directions: Break apart each word. Write the prefix and its meaning, the base word, and a simple definition for each word. An example has been done for you.

word	prefix means	base word	definition
❶ construct	*con-* = with, together	*struct* = build	to build something by putting it together
❷ contraction		*tract* = pull, draw, drag	
❸ cooperate		*oper* = work	
❹ coauthor			
❺ coexist			
❻ copilot			

Name: _____   Date: _____

Combine and Create:
Prefixes *co-* and *con-*

Directions: Add the prefix *co-* or *con-* to the bases. Then, write out the entire *co-* or *con-* word next to the most fitting statement.

co-/con- + _____
traction   struction   author   operate exist   ductor   star

Statement	Word
❶ Someone who writes a book with another person	
❷ A word that uses an apostrophe to connect two different words—for example, turning "is not" into "isn't"	
❸ When cats and dogs live together peacefully in one house	
❹ Working together to get a job done	
❺ Movie stars who act together in a TV show	
❻ Someone who waves a baton in front of a symphony orchestra to make the musicians play music together	
❼ Building something by putting pieces together	

Name: _____ Date: _____

Read and Reason:
Prefixes *co-* and *con-*

Directions: Read the passage. Circle the words with the directional prefixes *co-* and *con-*. Then, answer the questions.

Passage A

Our Class Publishing Company

Our class decided to start a publishing company. We wanted to make books of our writing. We were proud of ourselves as writers!

First, we needed to make some rules for our company. Our teacher, Ms. Sanchez, said we could figure out the rules by ourselves. Some kids suggested rules. Then, we tried to reach a consensus on the rules. If reaching a consensus wasn't possible, we voted. Here are our rules:

- Topics: Any topics are fine. We can write stories, poems, plays, reports, or even song lyrics. We can also write directions, such as how to construct something.

- Pieces of writing can be illustrated or coillustrated. They can also be published without illustrations.

- Pieces of writing can have a single author, coauthors, or multiple authors. If pieces are cowritten, all authors' names should appear.

- We will make committees to duplicate the books and make bindings for them.

What do you think of the company rules? Did they forget any?
Do you think the rules will work?

Name: _____ Date: _____

Read and Reason:
Prefixes *co-* and *con-* (cont.)

Directions: Read the passage. Circle the words with the directional prefixes *co-* and *con-*. Then, answer the questions.

Passage B

Employee-Owned Companies

If workers do the work, should they also get the profits? This is the idea behind employee-owned companies. These are sometimes called *worker cooperatives*. Employees own voting shares in the company. Sometimes they buy these voting shares. Other times, they are part of employees' pay. Employees can vote on lots of company-related issues.

Most employee-owned businesses connect to one another through groups like the Small Business Association. This way they can learn from each other.

You might think that only very small businesses are employee-owned. Some huge companies are, too. Employees own construction companies, supermarkets, and sports stores companies, for example. The number of employees can range from just a few to thousands.

Many economists believe that employee-owned companies are a good idea. Workers may do a better job when they know they own the company.

Do you think employee-owned companies are a good idea? Why or why not? Would you like to run your own company? What kind of company would you like to run?

Name: _____ Date: _____

Review:
Crossword Puzzle

Directions: Fill in the crossword puzzle on the next page with words from the Word Bank. Use the sentences to help you.

Word Bank				
contract	cooperate	coworker	defrost	deplane
descend	exhale	exit	explode	predict
preheat	preview	submarine	subway	subzero

Across

3 We live on the fourth floor, so I must _____ many stairs to get outside.

5 We have a new _____ freezer. It keeps ice cream really cold!

6 Everyone will _____ to clean up the city park.

10 The new pitcher signed a _____ to play for my favorite ball team.

11 My dad and his _____ drive to work together.

13 Would you be afraid to go underwater in a _____?

Down

1 I wish I knew how to _____ the weather.

2 Our Thanksgiving turkey is frozen. It will take a long time to _____.

3 The plane was big and crowded. It took a long time for us to _____.

4 The doctor listened to my chest and asked me to inhale and _____.

7 During the fire drill, we had to _____ the building quickly.

8 The fireworks will begin to _____ at 9:30 p.m.

9 Recipes work best if you _____ the oven.

12 I'm excited to see the new movie. The _____ looked great!

13 When we go to the city, I love to ride the _____.

Name: _____   Date: _____

Review:

Crossword Puzzle *(cont.)*

Prefixes *uni-* and *unit-*

Standards: Uses a variety of sentence structures to expand and embed ideas (McREL 2.3)
Uses conventions of spelling in written compositions (McREL 3.7)
Uses phonetic and structural analysis techniques, syntactic structure, and semantic context to decode unknown words (McREL 5.4)

Materials

- *Divide and Conquer: Prefixes uni- and unit-* (page 103)

- *Combine and Create: Prefixes uni- and unit-* (page 104)

- *Read and Reason: Prefixes uni- and unit-* (pages 105–106)

Teaching Tips

- The prefixes *uni-* and *unit-* mean "one" or "single."

- *Uni-* attaches both to intact words (*unicycle*) and to Latin bases that are not intact words (e.g., *unify*). A *base* is a unit of meaning that gives the main idea, or basic meaning, of the word. It can be a whole word (*uniform*) or a word part (*unify*).

- In some words, *uni-* or *unit-* does not attach to anything. When that happens, *uni-* or *unit-* acts as a base because it provides the word's basic meaning (e.g., *unit, unite, unique, union*).

- When reading silently, some students may initially confuse this prefix with the negative prefix *un-* (presented in Unit II, Lesson 3). This confusion can be avoided by having students pronounce the words aloud. The numerical prefixes *uni-* and *unit-* are pronounced like *you* (long /u/). In contrast, the negative prefix *un-* is pronounced to rhyme with *bun* (short /u/). The Combine and Create exercise provides practice in sorting negative *un-* words from *uni-* and *unit-* words meaning "one" or "single."

Guided Practice

Activate Background Knowledge

1. Ask students to raise their hands if they know how to ride a bicycle. Ask students whether they started learning how to ride a bike on a two-wheeler. Ask students how many wheels their first bikes had. You may get the response, "three." Point out that bikes with three wheels are called *tricycles*. Write the word *tricycle* on the board. Put a slash between *tri-* and *cycle*. Explain that *tri-* is a prefix meaning "three"; a *tricycle* has three wheels. Now write the word *bicycle* on the board. Put a slash between *bi-* and *cycle*. Ask students how many wheels a bicycle has. Invite their responses and support those who answer "two." Ask them what they think the prefix *bi-* means. Tells students that *bi-* means "two."

2. Now, ask, "If a tricycle has three wheels and a bicycle has two wheels, how many wheels does a *unicycle* have?" Write *unicycle* on the board. Put a slash between *uni-* and *cycle*. Invite student responses and support those who answer that a unicycle has "one" wheel. Explain to students that in a circus, they might see a clown riding a one-wheeled cycle, called a *unicycle*. Tell students that *uni-* is a prefix meaning "one" or "single."

Prefixes *uni-* and *unit-* (cont.)

3. Tell students that in all words beginning with the prefix *uni-* or *unit-*, the beginning sound is pronounced like the long /u/ in the word *you*. Write a few more *uni-* or *unit-* words on the board and ask students to say them out loud, emphasizing the long /u/ sounds: *United* States of America, a school *uniform*, a mythical *unicorn*, etc. Ask students, "How does each of these *uni-* or *unit-* words mean 'one'?" (*The* United *States is "one" or a "single" nation out of many states; a* uniform *is a "single" or "one" type of clothing worn by people in a profession; a* unicorn *has a "single" or "one" horn*.)

4. As a class, discuss the meaning of *uni-* and *unit-*, noting how these prefixes do not mean the same as negative prefix *un-*. If students confuse *uni-* and *unit-* with the negative prefix *un-*, write the word *unable* on the board. Ask students to say the word aloud. Point out that in all words beginning with the prefix *un-*, the beginning sound is pronounced like the short /u/ in *bun*. Remind students that it is often helpful to pronounce *uni-* and *unit-* words aloud and then ask themselves, "How does this word mean 'one' or 'single'?"

5. Invite students to generate additional *uni-* or *unit-* words. If they need assistance, use the following sentences as prompts:

   - Each one of you is individual and special. No one in the world is exactly like anyone else. Each person is _____. (*unique*)

   - When a choir sings, all of the voices come together to sound like one voice. They are singing in _____. (*unison*)

   - When people work together to solve a problem, they act as one group. They are _____. (*united*)

Divide and Conquer

6. Distribute the *Divide and Conquer: Prefixes uni-* and *unit-* activity sheet (page 103) to students. Guide students through the activity sheet. Starting with the first word, *unicorn*, explain, "If the base *corn* means 'horn' and the prefix *uni-* means 'one, single,' then *unicorn* means 'one horn.'" As students work through this activity, stop occasionally to reinforce how *uni-* is different from the negative prefix *un-*. Ask students how to tell if a word contains *uni-* or *un-* (pronunciation and context of word and text).

Combine and Create

7. Distribute the *Combine and Create: Prefixes uni-* and *unit-* activity sheet (page 104) to students. Have students work in pairs to solve the riddles. All words will begin with *uni-*. When students complete the activity, have them create their own *uni-* word riddles. Provide time for students to solve one another's riddles because talking about and playing with words help students master difficult vocabulary.

Read and Reason

8. Distribute the *Read and Reason: Prefixes uni-* and *unit-* activity sheets (pages 105–106) to students. Have students read one or both passages and answer the comprehension questions on a separate sheet of paper. Ask students to circle the *uni-* and *unit-* words they find. If the passages are too difficult for independent reading, ask students to read in pairs or follow along as you read aloud. If you read the passage to them, tell them to raise their hands when they hear a *uni-* or *unit-* word. After they (or you) have finished reading, discuss the passage. Ask student volunteers to identify compound words and explain their meaning.

Prefixes *uni-* and *unit-* (cont.)

Extend and Explore

Choose from among the activities located in Appendix B to give students extra practice with the numerical prefixes *uni-* and *unit-*.

Answer Key

Divide and Conquer: Prefixes *uni-* and *unit-* (page 103)

Students' answers for the "definition" section may vary; accept a range of answers.

1. unicorn: one, single; horn; an imaginary animal with one horn
2. unify: one, single; make; to make a group of people act as one
3. uniform: one, single; shape; to have one form/shape look the same, as in clothing
4. union: one, single; concept; a single and undivided concept or idea
5. unicycle: one, single; wheel; a bike with one wheel
6. unit: one, single; thing; a single thing, object, person, or group

Combine and Create: Prefixes *uni-* and *unit-* (page 104)

1. unique
2. United States
3. unicycle
4. unison
5. union
6. universe

Students' riddles will vary.

Read and Reason: Prefixes *uni-* and *unit-* (pages 105–106)

Passage A: *unicorn, uniform, uniforms, united, unanimous, unison*

Students' answers will vary.

Passage B: *United, unique, unification, union, Union, unanimous, reunification, reunited*

Students' answers will vary.

Name: _____   Date: _____

Divide and Conquer:
Prefixes *uni-* and *unit-*

Directions: Break apart each word. Write the prefix and its meaning and a simple definition for each word. An example has been done for you.

word	prefix means	base word	definition
❶ unicorn	*uni-* = one, single	*corn* = horn	an imaginary animal with one horn
❷ unify		*fy* = make, do	
❸ uniform		*form* = form, shape	
❹ union		*-ion* (suffix) = concept	
❺ unicycle		*cycl* = wheel, circle	
❻ unit		*-it* (suffix) = thing	

Name: _____ Date: _____

Combine and Create:
Prefixes *uni-* and *unit-*

Directions: Use the clues to figure out the *uni-* words. If you work as a unit with your partner, you'll be able to outsmart the riddler!

Word Bank					
unique	United States	unicycle	union	unison	universe

❶ I am "one of a kind." I rhyme with "you sneak." There is no one like me!
_____

❷ I am a country. I am in North America. I have 50 states that are all connected.
_____

❸ You might ride me if your bicycle has a flat tire. I get around on my own.
_____

❹ I like people being together. When people work the way I do, they can get more done. _____

❺ I am what happens when people come together to form one group. Abraham Lincoln tried to keep all the states in one of me. _____

❻ I am vast. The planets and stars turn in me. There is only one of me, but I am endless. _____

Directions: Write a riddle for your favorite *uni-* or *unit-* word. Then, challenge a partner to solve your riddle.

Clue 1: _____

Clue 2: _____

Clue 3: _____

My *uni-* or *unit-* word is _____.

Name: _____   Date: _____

Read and Reason:
Prefixes *uni-* and *unit-*

Directions: Read the passage. Circle the words with the numerical prefixes *uni-* and *unit-*. Then, answer the question.

Passage A

Our School's Dress Code

Our school's mascot is the unicorn. That mascot is just right. The unicorn has only one horn. Our school requires all students to wear a uniform. All the boys and all the girls must dress in one clothing style. Many students do not like uniforms. Some teachers tell us that the uniforms show we are a united school. We talked to our teacher about this. He suggested that we take a poll of fourth graders' feelings about the school dress code.

We asked every fourth grader how he or she felt about the school uniform policy. Students' feelings about it were unanimous. They want our school to adopt a more flexible dress code. They want to wear a greater variety of clothing.

We wanted to speak to our principal in unison about the poll results. But our class chose five students to tell her our ideas about the school dress code instead. The principal listened to our ideas. She said she would talk with teachers, parents, and other students. Two weeks later, we heard the good news. Our dress code proposal was accepted!

What reasons could the fourth graders use to
change the school dress code?

Name: _____ Date: _____

Read and Reason:
Prefixes *uni-* and *unit-* (cont.)

Directions: Read the passage. Circle the words with the numerical prefixes *uni-* and *unit-*. Then, answer the question.

Passage B

America's Civil War

The United States is unique in many ways. When it was founded in 1776, it was the only country with a government that the citizens chose. The United States had no king or queen. Instead, people elected others to represent them in the government. The United States was also formed by the unification of separate states. It was a union of states.

This all changed in 1861. The Civil War began when the Southern states left the Union. The Southern states started a new country called the Confederacy. Not all people in the Confederacy were unanimous in their wish to leave the Union. Still, most felt that the Southern states had the right to leave the United States. The Northern states felt differently. Northerners thought the unification of 1776 was permanent. The United States could never be divided. States could not leave the Union.

The war took more than three years. Finally, the Union army won the war. Then, reunification began. The Northern and Southern states were reunited. America was made whole again.

> What do you think are some of the reasons the Southern states wanted to leave the Union?

Prefix *bi-*

Standards: Uses a variety of sentence structures to expand and embed ideas (McREL 2.3)
Uses conventions of spelling in written compositions (McREL 3.7)
Uses phonetic and structural analysis techniques, syntactic structure, and semantic context to decode unknown words (McREL 5.4)

Materials

- *Divide and Conquer: Prefix bi-* (page 109)
- *Combine and Create: Prefix bi-* (page 110)
- *Read and Reason: Prefix bi-* (pages 111–112)

Teaching Tips

- The prefix *bi-* means "two."

- *Bi-* attaches to both whole words (*bicycle*) and to Latin bases that are not whole words (*bisect*). A *base* is a unit of meaning that gives the main idea, or basic meaning, of the word. It can be a whole word (*bimonthly*) or a word part (*binoculars*).

- The meanings of the Latin bases used in this lesson are provided. The objective is for students to internalize the meaning of the prefix *bi-* while working with words that deal with familiar concepts.

Guided Practice · · · · · · · · · · · ·

Activate Background Knowledge

1. If you taught Lesson 13: Prefixes *uni-* and *unit-*, remind students of the discussion you had about bicycles during the *uni-* lesson. Write the word *bicycle* on the board, putting a slash between *bi-* and *cycle*. Ask students how many wheels a bicycle has. Then, ask what the prefix *bi-* means (*two*).

2. Ask students to raise their hands if they know how to speak more than one language. Write the word *bilingual* on the board. Put a slash between *bi-* and *lingual*. Explain to students that if they know how to speak two languages, they are *bilingual*. Explain that *lingu* is a Latin base that means "language," so *bilingual* literally means "having two languages."

3. Next, ask students to generate other *bi-* words they know. If they need assistance, use the following sentences as prompts:

   - I have the newspaper delivered to my house twice a week. It is delivered _____. (*biweekly*)

   - I have tickets to the baseball game, but my seat is all the way at the back of the stadium. I will need _____ to see the game. (*binoculars*)

   - In science class, we have to cut the flower stems into two parts so we can look inside. We have to _____ the flower. (*bisect*)

Prefix *bi-* *(cont.)*

Divide and Conquer

4. Distribute the *Divide and Conquer: Prefix bi-* activity sheet (page 109) to students. Guide students through the activity sheet. Students work with words in which *bi-* attaches to both Latin bases and intact words. The meanings of the Latin bases have been provided.

Combine and Create

5. Distribute the *Combine and Create: Prefix bi-* activity sheet (page 110) to students. Ask students to work in pairs to sort the words into two lists: those in which *bi-* means "two" and those in which it does not. Remind students of the importance of both meaning and context when determining whether a word contains a prefix or just a combination of letters (e.g., *bi-* as in *bilingual*, and *bi* as in *bib*). After students sort the words, have them share their answers as a class. Have students explain how they knew whether a word paired with *bi-*. Talking about words and strategies used to determine their meaning is a powerful way to help students build vocabulary knowledge and word analysis skills. Then, have students illustrate the sentences.

Read and Reason

6. Distribute the *Read and Reason: Prefix bi-* activity sheets (pages 111–112) to students. Have students read one or both passages and answer the comprehension questions on a separate sheet of paper. Ask students to circle the *bi-* words they find. If the passages are too difficult for independent reading, ask students to read in pairs or follow along as you read aloud. If you read the passage to them, tell them to raise their hands when they hear a *bi-* word. After they (or you) have finished reading, discuss the passage. Ask student volunteers to identify *bi-* words and explain their meaning.

Extend and Explore

Choose from among the activities located in Appendix B to give students extra practice with the numerical prefix *bi-*.

Answer Key

Divide and Conquer: Prefix *bi-* (page 109)

Students' answers for the "definition" section may vary; accept a range of answers.

1. bicycle: two; wheel; a vehicle with two wheels
2. biannual: two; year; an event that occurs every two years or twice a year
3. bifocal: two; focus; eyeglasses that provide two foci—one up close and one farther away
4. bilingual: two; language; a person who speaks two languages
5. bisect: two; cut; to cut into two parts
6. binoculars: two; eye; a device to look through with two eyes and see things from far away

Combine and Create: Prefix *bi-* (page 110)

Part 1:

bi- means "two": *bicycle, biweekly, bifocal, biannual, biyearly, bimonthly, bisect, bilingual*

bi- doesn't mean "two": *biscuit, bite, bill, binder, bid, big, billion*

Part 2: Students' drawings will vary.

Read and Reason: Prefix *bi-* (pages 111–112)

Passage A: *bifocals, biplane, binoculars, bicycle, biceps*

Students' answers will vary.

Passage B: *bicameral, bipartisan, bicentennial, biannually*

Students' answers will vary.

Name: _____   Date: _____

Divide and Conquer:
Prefix *bi-*

Directions: Break apart each word. Write the prefix and its meaning, the base word, and a simple definition for each word. An example has been done for you.

word	prefix means	base word	definition
❶ bicycle	*bi-* = two	*cycl* = wheel	a vehicle with two wheels
❷ biannual		*annu* = year	
❸ bifocal		*foc* = focus	
❹ bilingual		*lingu* = language	
❺ bisect		*sect* = cut	
❻ binoculars		*ocul* = eye	

Name: _____   Date: _____

Combine and Create:
Prefix *bi-*

Directions: Sometimes *bi-* means "two," but sometimes it doesn't. When you remove the *bi-* prefix from a word, the base should make sense. If you do not have a meaningful base after you remove *bi-*, the word does NOT have the *bi-* prefix. Work with your partner to sort the words into the correct boxes. Remember to be on the lookout for the meaning of "two" in the words!

Word Bank					
biscuit	bite	bill	bicycle	biweekly	bifocal
binder	bid	biannual	biyearly	big	billion
bimonthly	bisect	bilingual			

bi- means "two"	*bi-* doesn't mean "two"

Directions: Draw a picture to show what is happening.

❶ Amelia Earhart flew over the Atlantic Ocean in a **biplane**! The plane was much smaller than today's planes. It also had two wings on either side of the plane.	
❷ The scientist **bisected** the plant stem to learn how it worked on the inside.	
❸ We live in a **bi-level** house. The living room is on the first level and the bedrooms are on the second level.	

Name: _____   Date: _____

Read and Reason:
Prefix _bi-_

Directions: Read the passage. Circle the words with the numerical prefix _bi-_.
Then, answer the question.

Passage A

A Mystery Plane

I couldn't believe what I was seeing! I had to take off my bifocals
and clean them again. Was I seeing a mirage? I put my clean
glasses back on. I was not dreaming. There in the sky was a 1918
biplane circling right above me.

I got out my binoculars to take a closer look. The plane was a
sight to behold—two main wings, one above the other. You don't
see too many of those planes today. When the plane landed in
the field down the road, I jumped on my bicycle and pedaled as
fast as I could to see the amazing machine up close. I got to the
parked plane just as the pilot was climbing down the ladder from the
cockpit. His large biceps told me that a pilot of such a plane had to
have strong arms to control it. I wonder if he might allow me to take
a ride with him on his next flight!

Why do you think older airplanes needed two wings to fly?

Name: _____ Date: _____

Read and Reason:
Prefix *bi-* *(cont.)*

Directions: Read the passage. Circle the words with the numerical prefix *bi-*. Then, answer the question.

Passage B

America's Government

Governments are important in our lives. The U.S. government has three branches. One is the executive. Another is the legislative. The third is the judicial. The legislative branch makes the laws. The president is in charge of the executive branch. The president is the executive. He or she carries out these laws. The judicial branch often decides if the laws are legal.

The legislative branch is bicameral. It is made up of two bodies, or houses. One is the House of Representatives. The other is the Senate. Most state governments have bicameral legislatures, too. Only Nebraska has a unicameral legislature.

New laws need bipartisan support. This means both political parties need to agree. For example, the United States celebrated its bicentennial in 1976. It was 200 years old! But bipartisan support was needed to pay for the celebrations. The legislative branch also makes budgets. These budgets tell governments how to spend money. The U.S. government and some states make budgets annually. A new budget is made every year. In other states, budgets are made biannually. Legislatures play a key role in the government.

How long does a biannual budget plan last?

Prefix *tri-*

Standards: Uses a variety of sentence structures to expand and embed ideas (McREL 2.3)

Uses conventions of spelling in written compositions (McREL 3.7)

Uses phonetic and structural analysis techniques, syntactic structure, and semantic context to decode unknown words (McREL 5.4)

Materials

- *Divide and Conquer: Prefix tri-* (page 115)

- *Combine and Create: Prefix tri-* (page 116)

- *Read and Reason: Prefix tri-* (pages 117–118)

Teaching Tips

- The prefix *tri-* means "three." Most students will readily recognize *trio, triplets, tricycle,* and *triangle.*

- *Tri-* attaches to both whole words (*tricycle*) and to Latin bases that are not whole words (*trilingual*). A *base* is a unit of meaning that gives the main idea, or basic meaning, of the word. It can be a whole word (tri*color*) or a word part (tri*pod*). Students work with words that contain Latin bases and intact words in this lesson. The meanings of the Latin bases are provided. The objective is for students to internalize the meaning of the prefix *tri-* while working with words that deal with familiar concepts.

Guided Practice ············

Activate Background Knowledge

1. If you taught Lesson 13: Prefixes *uni-* and *unit-* and Lesson 14: Prefix *bi-*, remind students of the discussions you had about bicycles during the *uni-* and *bi-* lessons. Ask them to recall the word for a bike with three wheels, the type of bike they may have used when first learning how to ride. Write the word *tricycle* on the board, putting a slash between *tri-* and *cycle*. Ask students how many wheels a tricycle has. Then, ask what the prefix *tri-* means. (*three*)

2. Next, draw a triangle on the board. Ask students how many angles the shape has. Then, ask them the name of the shape. Write the word *triangle* on the board. Put a slash between *tri-* and *angle* so students can see how the word is divided. Then, ask them to explain why this shape is called a *triangle*.

3. Invite students to share other *tri-* words they may know. If they need assistance, use the following sentences as prompts:

   - *The Lord of the Rings* series has three books and movies. Books and movies that tell stories in three parts are called _____. (*trilogies*)

   - The a cappella group consisted of three men and no instruments. They were a singing _____. (*trio*)

   - My friend has two brothers who look just like him. They were all born on the same day. They are _____. (*triplets*)

Prefix *tri-* (cont.)

Divide and Conquer

4. Distribute the *Divide and Conquer: Prefix tri-* activity sheet (page 115) to students. Guide students through the activity sheet. As each word is completed, ask a student to share and explain his or her definition.

Combine and Create

5. Distribute the *Combine and Create: Prefix tri-* activity sheet (page 116) to students. Have students work in pairs to solve the riddles. Allow time for students to create their own riddles and trade with partners. Playing with words and their concepts is a powerful way for students to build understanding.

Read and Reason

6. Distribute the *Read and Reason: Prefix tri-* activity sheets (pages 117–118) to students. Have students read one or both passages and answer the comprehension questions on a separate sheet of paper. Ask students to circle the *tri-* words they find. If the passages are too difficult for independent reading, ask students to read in pairs or follow along as you read aloud. If you read the passage to them, tell them to raise their hands when they hear a *tri-* word. After they (or you) have finished reading, discuss the passage. Ask student volunteers to identify *tri-* words and explain their meaning.

Extend and Explore

Choose from among the activities located in Appendix B to give students extra practice with the numerical prefix *tri-*.

Answer Key

Divide and Conquer: Prefix *tri-* (page 115)

Students' answers for the "definition" section may vary; accept a range of answers.

1. triangle: three; angle; a shape with three angles

2. tripod: three; foot; a device with three "feet" that holds a camera

3. trisect: three; cut; to cut into three parts

4. triplets: three; fold, multiply; three babies born at the same time; also babies born in a "threefold" multiple birth

5. triathlon: three; contest; a sporting contest with three events

6. tricycle: three; wheel; a bike with three wheels

Combine and Create: Prefix *tri-* (page 116)

1. triceratops

2. trident

3. tripod

Students' riddles will vary.

Read and Reason: Prefix *tri-* (pages 117–118)

Passage A: *triplets, triathlon, triangles, tripod, tricycles*

Students' answers will vary.

Passage B: *triple, triathlon, triathlete, triathlons, triceratops*

Students' answers will vary.

Name: _____   Date: _____

Divide and Conquer:
Prefix *tri-*

Directions: Break apart each word. Write the prefix and its meaning and a simple definition for each word. An example has been done for you.

word	prefix means	base word	definition
❶ triangle	*tri-* = three	angle	a shape with three angles
❷ tripod		*pod* = foot	
❸ trisect		*sect* = cut	
❹ triplets		*ple* = fold, multiply	
❺ triathlon		*athl* = contest	
❻ tricycle		*cycle* = wheel	

Name: _____ Date: _____

Combine and Create:
Prefix *tri-*

Directions: Use the clues to figure out which *tri-* word from the Work Bank the riddle describes.

Word Bank		
trident	triceratops	tripod

❶ I am extinct.

I lived in prehistoric times.

My three horns helped me defend myself from predators.

What am I? _____

❷ Neptune and Poseidon carry me.

I am useful for spearing fish.

I am also a brand of chewing gum.

What am I? _____

❸ I stand on three legs.

I sometimes hold a camera.

What am I? _____

Directions: Choose your favorite *tri-* word and write a riddle for it. Then, challenge a partner to solve your riddle.

Clue 1: _____

Clue 2: _____

Clue 3: _____

What am I? _____

Name: _____ Date: _____

Read and Reason:
Prefix *tri-*

Directions: Read the passage. Circle the words with the numerical prefix *tri-*.
Then, answer the question.

Passage A

Instant Family

Our next-door neighbor, Mrs. Marcus, just had triplets—Jim, Tim, and Tom. Can you imagine having three babies all the same age? Mom says raising three little boys is like doing a triathlon at home.

All the neighbors put on a party for Mr. and Mrs. Marcus and their new family. All the neighbors brought desserts. Mom thought it would be cute to cut the cookies into little triangles. Dad wanted to take pictures of the babies. He made sure to set his camera on a tripod so that the camera would stay still.

I thought the best gift was a set of three tricycles, one for each of the babies. The neighbors will have to look out when the boys become old enough to take to the sidewalks on those new wheels.

Why do you think the neighbors will have to be careful when
the babies learn to ride their tricycles?

Name: _____　Date: _____

Read and Reason:
Prefix *tri-* (cont.)

Directions: Read the passage. Circle the words with the numerical prefix *tri-*.
Then, answer the question.

Passage B

Three Sports in One

　　It is hard to hit a triple in baseball. But it is probably much harder to win a triathlon. The triathlon is one of the most demanding of all sports. It is a multi-sport event. It is made up of three sporting events. These are usually swimming, bicycling, and running. A triathlete must be skilled in each of these sports.

　　The Ironman is probably the most famous of all triathlons. To win, a triathlete must swim nearly $2\frac{1}{2}$ miles, finish a 112-mile bicycle race, and then compete in a marathon. A marathon is a running race of over 26 miles. Nowadays, Ironman winners can finish all three events in less than 9 hours. That is amazing! To win a triathlon you'll need the speed of a gazelle. You will also need the strength of a triceratops!

> If you could create your own personal triathlon, what
> three events would you include?

Prefixes *quart-* and *quadr-*

Standards: Uses a variety of sentence structures to expand and embed ideas (McREL 2.3)
Uses conventions of spelling in written compositions (McREL 3.7)
Uses phonetic and structural analysis techniques, syntactic structure, and semantic context to decode unknown words (McREL 5.4)

Materials

- *Divide and Conquer: Prefixes quart- and quadr-* (page 121)

- *Combine and Create: Prefixes quart- and quadr-* (page 122)

- *Read and Reason: Prefixes quart- and quadr-* (pages 123–124)

Teaching Tips

- The numerical prefixes *quart-* and *quadr-* mean "four" and also "one-fourth" (e.g., a gallon of milk is made up of "four" *quarts*, each of those *quarts* is "one-fourth" of a gallon). When explaining the meaning of these prefixes, emphasize that the idea of "four" or "one-fourth" can be four separate things (a *quartet* is made up of "four" people; a *quarter* is "one-fourth" of a dollar). *Quart-* and *quadr-* words are found particularly in mathematics vocabulary.

- These prefixes usually attach to Latin bases that are not whole words (e.g., *quadrilateral, quadruple*). While the bases may be unfamiliar, the concept of "four" should be familiar. The meanings of the Latin bases used in this lesson are provided. The objective is for students to internalize the meaning of *quart-* and *quadr-* while working with words that deal with familiar concepts.

Guided Practice ·············

Activate Background Knowledge

1. Write the words *quart, quarter,* and *quadrilateral* on the board. Show students a gallon container. Ask them how many *quarts* equals one gallon (*four quarts*). Write, "A gallon equals four quarts" next to the word *quart*. Then, show students a one-dollar bill. Ask them how many *quarters* equal one dollar (*four quarters*). Write, "A quarter equals one-fourth of a dollar" next to the word *quarter*. Then, draw a quadrilateral (a shape with four sides) on the board. Ask them how many sides a quadrilateral has (*four sides*). Write, "A quadrilateral has four sides" next to the word *quadrilateral*.

2. Ask students what the words *quarter, quart,* and *quadrilateral* have in common. Accept responses that note the shared meaning of "four" and the *quart-* or *quadr-* prefixes. Return to the words *quarter* and *quadrilateral* on the board. Put a slash between *quart-* and *er* and between *quadr-* and *lateral* to show how the words are divided. Explain that both *quart-* and *quadr-* mean "four." (You may choose to extend this by pointing out that *-er* in *quarter* is a suffix meaning "a thing that," so *quarter* literally means "a thing that is one of four equal parts.")

3. Next, ask students to generate other *quart-* or *quadr-* words they may know. If they need assistance, use the following sentences as prompts:

   - Three babies born at the same time are called *triplets*. Four babies born at the same time are called _____. (*quadruplets*)

Prefixes *quart-* and *quadr-* (cont.)

- The group consisted of four men singing. They are a _____. (*quartet*)

- A shape with four angles is a _____. (*quadrangle*)

Divide and Conquer

4. Distribute the *Divide and Conquer: Prefixes quart- and quadr-* activity sheet (page 121) to students. Guide students through the activity sheet. Students will be working with words that contain Latin bases. The meanings of bases have been provided.

Combine and Create

5. Distribute the *Combine and Create: Prefixes quart- and quadr-* activity sheet (page 122) to students. Ask students to work in pairs to match the words with the phrases that describe them. Then, have students label the pictures with the *quart-* and *quadr-* words they represent. After students complete the activities, allow time to share answers in a class discussion. Ask students to explain how the concept of "four" is represented in the words. Talking about new vocabulary with others is an effective way of mastering it.

Read and Reason

6. Distribute the *Read and Reason: Prefixes quart- and quadr-* activity sheets (pages 123–124) to students. Have students read one or both passages and answer the comprehension questions on a separate sheet of paper. Ask them to circle the *quart-* and *quadr-* words they find. If the passages are too difficult for independent reading, ask students to read in pairs or follow along as you read aloud. If you read the passage to them, tell them to raise their hands when they hear a *quart-* or *quadr-* word. After reading, discuss the passage. Ask student volunteers to identify *quart-* and *quadr-* words and explain their meaning.

Extend and Explore

Choose from among the activities located in Appendix B to give students extra practice with the numerical prefixes *quart-* and *quadr-*.

Answer Key

Divide and Conquer: Prefixes *quart-* and *quadr-* (page 121)

Students' answers for the "definition" section may vary; accept a range of answers.

1. quadrilateral: four; side; a shape with four sides
2. quart: four; no base; a container equal to one-fourth of a gallon
3. quarter: four; no base; a unit of money worth one fourth of a dollar
4. quadruple: four; fold, multiply; to multiply an amount by four
5. quadruplets: four; fold, multiply; a group of four babies born at the same time; also babies born in a "fourfold" multiple birth
6. quadruped: four; foot; an animal with four feet

Combine and Create: Prefixes *quart-* and *quadr-* (page 122)

Part 1:

1. D   2. A   3. B   4. C

Part 2:

1. quadrilateral   3. quartet
2. quadriceps   4. quadruplets

Read and Reason: Prefixes *quart-* and *quadr-* (pages 123–124)

Passage A: *quarters, quartet, quarts, Quart, quadrilateral, quadriceps, quad, quadruplets*

$4.00

Passage B: *quadrants, quadriceps, quart*

Students' answers will vary.

Name: _____ Date: _____

Divide and Conquer:
Prefixes *quart-* and *quadr-*

Directions: Break apart each word. Write the prefix and its meaning, the base word, and a simple definition for each word. An example has been done for you.

word	prefix means	base word	definition
❶ quadrilateral	*quadr-* = four	*later-* = side	a shape with four sides
❷ quart		no base	
❸ quarter		no base	
❹ quadruple		*ple* = fold, multiply	
❺ quadruplets		*ple* = fold, multiply	
❻ quadruped		*ped* = foot	

Name: _____ Date: _____

Combine and Create:
Prefixes *quart-* and *quadr-*

Directions: Match the words with the correct answer.

❶ quadrilingual

❷ quart

❸ quadrupeds

❹ quarter

A. Four of me equals one gallon.

B. Animals with four feet belong to this group.

C. Four of me equals one dollar.

D. My sister speaks four languages. She is this.

Directions: Use the Word Bank to label each picture.

Word Bank			
quartet	quadrilateral	quadriceps	quadruplets

❶ _____

❷ _____

❸ _____

❹ _____

Name: _____ Date: _____

Read and Reason:
Prefixes *quart-* and *quadr-*

Directions: Read the passage. Circle the words with the numerical prefixes *quart-* and *quadr-*. Then, answer the question.

Passage A

Know Your Fours

Know your fours!

Four quarters make a dollar

Four singers a quartet

Four quarts make a gallon

Quart means "four," I'll bet.

Four sides make a quadrilateral

Four muscles make quadriceps

Now I know that *quad* means "four"

How many babies make quadruplets?

If you have a dollar and quadruple it, how much money will you have?

Name: _____ Date: _____

Read and Reason:
Prefixes *quart-* and *quadr-* (cont.)

Directions: Read the passage. Circle the words with the numerical prefixes *quart-* and *quadr-*. Then, answer the question.

Passage B

Build and Maintain Your Body

Regular exercise keeps your body strong. When exercising, be sure to involve all parts of your body. One way to make sure that all parts of your body get enough exercise is by dividing your body into quadrants. First is the upper body. This includes your shoulder, back, and arm muscles. Second is the lower body. Included here are your leg muscles, such as your quadriceps. Third is the core. The core muscles include your abdominals and hips. The final muscle is the heart. The heart is perhaps the most important muscle in your body.

You should exercise each of the four areas regularly, at least two to three times per week. Be sure that you start slowly when beginning your exercise program. It is also important to stay well hydrated when exercising. You will sweat and lose fluids when you exercise. Some experts suggest that for each workout, a person should drink a quart or more of water. Exercise is the key to a healthy body. However, you need to be smart when starting an exercise program.

Why do you think the author says that the heart is the most important muscle in your body?

Prefix *multi-*

Standards: Uses a variety of sentence structures to expand and embed ideas (McREL 2.3)
Uses conventions of spelling in written compositions (McREL 3.7)
Uses phonetic and structural analysis techniques, syntactic structure, and semantic context to decode unknown words (McREL 5.4)

Materials

- *Divide and Conquer: Prefix multi-* (page 128)

- *Combine and Create: Prefix multi-* (page 129)

- *Read and Reason: Prefix multi-* (pages 130–131)

Teaching Tips

- The prefix *multi-* means "many." It attaches to whole words (e.g., *multicolored, multicultural*) and to Latin bases that are not whole words (e.g., *multiply*). Remember that the objective is for students to learn that *multi-* means "many."

- Students may be familiar with the prefix *multi-* from commercial advertising. Many advertisers attach it to already existing words to attract customer attention, as in the words *multivitamin* and *multipurpose*.

- The words *multiply* and *multiplication* also contain the prefix *multi-*. The Latin base *ply* means "fold." To *multiply* means to increase two sets of numbers by "folding" them together. This concept is abstract and may be new to some students, making a discussion of the word *multiply* challenging. If you do not feel that this discussion is appropriate for your students, simply confirm that *multiply* and *multiplication* contain the *multi-* prefix. Then, ask students how these words represent the concept of "more."

Guided Practice · · · · · · · · · · · · ·

Activate Background Knowledge

1. Begin by asking students about their special talents. Ask students to raise their hands if they are talented at singing. Then, ask students to raise their hands if they are talented at playing sports. Repeat this process with a few other talents (e.g., dancing, playing an instrument, etc.). Point out that the class has many talents. Then, write the word *multitalented* on the board.

2. Next, demonstrate the idea of *multimillionaire*. For example, tell students that Donald Trump (or another wealthy individual students are familiar with) has "many" millions of dollars. He is a multimillionaire. Write the word *multimillionaire* on the board. Ask students what the words *multitalented* and *multimillionaire* have in common. Accept responses that take note of the shared meaning of "many" and the *multi-* prefix.

3. Tell students that *multi-* is a prefix meaning "many." Return to the words *multitalented* and *multimillionaire* on the board. Put a slash between *multi-* and the base words to show students how the words are built.

Prefix *multi-* *(cont.)*

4. Next, ask students to generate other *multi-* words they may know. If they need assistance, use the following sentences as prompts:

   - A shape with three sides is called a *trilateral* shape. A shape with four sides is called a *quadrilateral*. A shape with many sides is called a _____. (*multilateral*)

   - A Swiss Army knife has many purposes. It can cut fabric, open cans, and slice wood. It is a _____ tool. (*multipurpose*)

   - Every morning, I take a vitamin that has many nutrients, not just one. I take a _____. (*multivitamin*)

Divide and Conquer

5. Distribute the *Divide and Conquer: Prefix multi-* activity sheet (page 128) to students. Guide students through the activity sheet. Some words contain Latin bases. Their meanings are provided.

Combine and Create

6. Distribute the *Combine and Create: Prefix multi-* activity sheet (page 129) to students. Ask students to work in pairs to solve the word riddles. After students solve the riddles, have them share answers as a class. Have students discuss how the words represent the concept of "many."

Read and Reason

7. Distribute the *Read and Reason: Prefix multi-* activity sheets (pages 130–131) to students. Have students read one or both passages and answer the comprehension questions on a separate sheet of paper. Ask students to circle the *multi-* words they find. If the passages are too difficult for independent reading, ask students to read in pairs or follow along as you read aloud. If you read the passage to them, tell them to raise their hands when they hear a *multi-* word. After they (or you) have finished reading, discuss the passage. Ask student volunteers to identify *multi-* words and explain their meanings.

Extend and Explore

Choose from among the activities located in Appendix B to give students extra practice with the numerical prefix *multi-*.

Prefix *multi-* *(cont.)*

Answer Key

Divide and Conquer: Prefix *multi-* (page 128)

Students' answers for the "definition" section may vary; accept a range of answers.

1. multivitamin: many; vitamin; a vitamin containing many vitamins

2. multimedia: many; media; using many different kinds of media, such as text, video, still pictures, and audio representations

3. multilingual: many; language; able to speak many languages

4. multimillionaire; many; millionaire; a person who has many millions of dollars

5. multitalented: many; talented; having many talents

6. multicolored: many; color; something having many colors

Combine and Create: Prefix *multi-* (page 129)

1. multicolored
2. multivitamin
3. multitasker
4. multitalented
5. multilingual

Read and Reason: Prefix *multi-* (pages 130–131)

Passage A: *multimillionaire, multidimensional, multinational, multitasking, multistory, multivitamin*

Students' answers will vary.

Passage B: *Multinational, multicultural, multilingual*

Students' answers will vary.

Scrambles (page 132)

Part 1:

1. multipurpose
2. triplets
3. bisect
4. uniforms

Part 2: Students' answers will vary.

Divide and Conquer:
Prefix *multi-*

Directions: Break apart each word. Write the prefix and its meaning, the base word, and a simple definition for each word. An example has been done for you.

word	prefix means	base word	definition
1 multivitamin	*multi-* = many	vitamin	a vitamin containing many vitamins
2 multimedia			
3 multilingual		*lingu* = language	
4 multimillionaire			
5 multitalented			
6 multicolored			

Name: _____   Date: _____

Combine and Create:
Prefix *multi-*

Directions: Use the clues to solve the riddles. Use the Word Bank to help you.

Word Bank				
multilingual	multicolored	multivitamin	multitasker	multitalented

❶ I describe rainbows, flowers, and paintings.

I will never be just black and white.

I love it when all the colors come together!

What am I? _____

❷ You might take me in the morning.

I keep you healthy and strong.

Vitamins C, B, E, and even calcium are in me.

What am I? _____

❸ I like to get many tasks done at once.

Talking on the phone while washing the dishes is an example of me.

Sometimes I can be distracted and make mistakes.

What am I? _____

❹ I describe a person who can sing, dance, and play an instrument well.

Someone like me has a good chance of winning a talent show.

What am I? _____

❺ I speak many languages.

I can communicate with people from many cultures.

You may have to study for a long time to be like me.

What am I? _____

Name: _____   Date: _____

Read and Reason:
Prefix *multi-*

Directions: Read the passage. Circle the words with the numerical prefix *multi-*. Then, answer the question.

Passage A

How to Make Millions

My friend Mark wants to become a multimillionaire. He likes money. He already has a multidimensional plan for reaching his goal. First, he will earn a college degree in business. Then, he will get a job with a multinational computer company. He plans to work his way up to better and better jobs. He knows it will take a lot of hard work and much multitasking to achieve his goal. He wants an office on the top floor of a multistory building. When he gets there, I will visit him. But now he's only in fourth grade. So I think it's probably best for my friend to study hard and take his multivitamin every morning.

> What does Mark mean when he says he will have to multitask to achieve his goal?

Name: _____   Date: _____

Read and Reason:
Prefix *multi-* (cont.)

Directions: Read the passage. Circle the words with the numerical prefix *multi-*.
Then, answer the question.

Passage B

Appreciating Those Who Are Different

We live in a world that seems to be getting smaller. People speaking
different languages and from different cultures are meeting one another.
Young people in China come to the United States to study at American
universities. Multinational businesses can be found in many countries.

Our world is shrinking. So we must develop a multicultural view of the
world. This means that we need to respect people who come from cultures
different from our own. Rather than think of such people as different, we
need to learn about and value their customs and cultures.

More schools are stressing the
importance of students becoming
multilingual. Today's successful people
can talk to others who speak different
languages. A person who can speak and
read English, Spanish, and Chinese will
have an advantage over someone who
only speaks one language.

Developing a greater understanding
of others is worth the effort. We can
appreciate and respect others who are
different from us. Then, the world can
become a kinder and more peaceful place for everyone.

Explain what the author means by saying the world is getting
smaller or shrinking. Is it becoming smaller in size?

Name: _____ Date: _____

Review:
Scrambles

Part I

Directions: Unscramble the letters to make a word that fits in the sentence.

❶ **Scrambled word:** eilmopprstuu

My mom uses _____ cleaner. It works on glass, wood, and plastic.

❷ **Scrambled word:** eilprstt

A few weeks ago, our friends Bill and Stephanie went from no children to three children. They had _____.

❸ **Scrambled word:** bceist

If you _____ a pizza, two parts should be the same size.

❹ **Scrambled word:** fimnorsu

My dad and all the other nurses at the hospital wear _____ each day.

Part II

Directions: Choose three words from the Word Bank. Then, scramble the words like those in Part I. Challenge a classmate to unscramble your words.

Word Bank				
biweekly	multicolored	quarter	triangle	unicycle

Scrambled word: _____ **Unscrambled word:** _____

Scrambled word: _____ **Unscrambled word:** _____

Scrambled word: _____ **Unscrambled word:** _____

Suffix -less

Standards: Uses a variety of sentence structures to expand and embed ideas (McREL 2.3)
Uses conventions of spelling in written compositions (McREL 3.7)
Uses phonetic and structural analysis techniques, syntactic structure, and semantic context to decode unknown words (McREL 5.4)

Materials

- *Divide and Conquer: Suffix -less* (page 136)
- *Combine and Create: Suffix -less* (page 137)
- *Read and Reason: Suffix -less* (pages 138–139)

Teaching Tips

- This unit introduces familiar and widely used suffixes. The suffix *-less*, which means "without," is the focus of this lesson.

- A suffix is a word part that comes at the end of a word and changes its meaning. For example, a *seedless* watermelon is a watermelon "without" seeds. Likewise, a *sleepless* night is a night "without" sleep.

- Suffixes can be added to whole words or to Latin bases. All of the suffixes in this unit, however, are added to whole words that should be familiar to most students. It may be helpful to present each suffix with an introductory hyphen (e.g., *-less*). This may help students visualize that a suffix begins after the base of a word.

- When explaining the meaning of a word with a suffix, the meaning of the suffix should always come first in the definition, even though the suffix is at the end of the word. For example, *careless* means "without care," not "care without." As students offer definitions for words with suffixes, you may need to emphasize that their definitions must always make sense.

- When *-less* is added to the end of a word, the spelling of that word does not change (e.g., *hope, hopeless; care, careless*).

Guided Practice

Activate Background Knowledge

1. Ask students to identify some of the prefixes they have studied (e.g., *un-, re-, in-, ex-, sub-*). Ask them what these prefixes do when attached to the bases of words *(change its meaning; negate; give direction)*. Tell them that they will now learn about *suffixes*. Ask, "If a **prefix** comes at the beginning of a word, where might a **suffix** come?" Explain that just like a prefix, a suffix also changes a word's meaning.

2. Explain that many words with prefixes also have suffixes. Most of the words learned in school contain three roots: prefix, base, and suffix. Emphasize that both prefixes and suffixes change the meaning of the word.

Suffix -*less* (cont.)

3. Ask students to raise their hands if they like to eat watermelon (or grapes). Then, ask them if they prefer to eat watermelon (or grapes) with or without seeds. Tell students that if they prefer to eat watermelon (or grapes) without seeds, then they enjoy *seedless* watermelon (or grapes). Write the word *seedless* on the board.

4. Ask students to raise their hands if they have ever stayed up very late at night and felt tired the next day. Ask students why they felt tired. Accept answers that have to do with the idea of being "without" sleep. Write the word *sleepless* on the board.

5. Ask students what *seedless* and *sleepless* have in common. Accept answers that refer to the idea of "without" and the -*less* suffix. Tell students that -*less* is a suffix. It comes at the end of the word and changes the meaning of the word to "without." Put a slash between the -*less* suffix and the base words in both *seedless* and *sleepless* to show students how the words are built.

6. Ask students to generate other words they may know with the -*less* suffix. If students need assistance, use the following sentences as prompts:

   • The food was bland and boring. It didn't taste like anything. It was _____. (*tasteless*)

   • Superheroes are really brave. When they battle villains, they have no fear. They are _____. (*fearless*)

   • I like to chew gum, but my dentist says the sugar is bad for my teeth. She recommends _____ gum. (*sugarless*)

Divide and Conquer

7. Distribute the *Divide and Conquer: Suffix -less* activity sheet (page 136) to students. As students Divide and Conquer, provide time for them to discuss how the words represent the idea of "without." Have students offer examples that demonstrate the meaning of the words (e.g., as students Divide and Conquer *colorless*, ask them to think of colorless objects). This is an effective strategy for helping students internalize the meaning of the suffix.

8. For this Divide and Conquer, students work with bases that are intact words. They divide the words by first defining the meaning of the base, followed by the meaning of the suffix. When putting together the meaning of the word, however, the suffix comes first. For example, *hopeless* is divided as "hope + without," but the word means "without hope," not "hope without."

Combine and Create

9. Distribute the *Combine and Create: Suffix -less* activity sheet (page 137) to students. Students work with partners to solve word riddles. As students complete the riddles, allow time for a class discussion about the strategies students used to solve the riddles. For this Combine and Create, students create their own riddles for words with the *less*- suffix. Allow time for students to solve each other's riddles. Creating and solving riddles for vocabulary concepts is an engaging way for students to master abstract concepts. Talking about words and their meanings helps students to learn new vocabulary.

Suffix -less (cont.)

Read and Reason

10. Distribute the *Read and Reason: Suffix -less* activity sheets (pages 138–139) to students. Have students read one or both passages and answer the comprehension questions on a separate sheet of paper. Ask them to circle the -less words they find. If the passages are too difficult for independent reading, ask students to read in pairs or follow along as you read aloud. Tell them to raise their hands when they hear a word with the -less suffix. Circle the words they identify. After you have finished reading, discuss the passage. Return to each of the -less words and ask student volunteers to explain their meaning.

Extend and Explore

Choose from among the activities located in Appendix B to give students extra practice with the suffix -less.

Answer Key

Divide and Conquer: Suffix -less (page 136)

Students' answers for the "definition" section may vary; accept a range of answers.

1. colorless: without; color; without color
2. joyless: without; joy; without joy
3. homeless: without; home; without a home
4. sleepless: without; sleep; without sleep
5. wireless: without; wire; without wires
6. seedless: without; seed; without seeds

Combine and Create: Suffix -less (page 137)

1. joyless
2. colorless
3. powerless
4. seedless
5. wireless
6. homeless

Read and Reason: Suffix -less (pages 138–139)

Passage A: *clueless, penniless, tireless, priceless*

Students' answers will vary.

Passage B: *clueless, relentless, tireless, countless, airless, breathless*

Students' answers will vary.

Name: _____ Date: _____

Divide and Conquer:
Suffix *-less*

Directions: Break apart each word. Write the suffix and its meaning, the base word, and a simple definition for each word. An example has been done for you.

word	suffix means	base word	definition
❶ colorless	*-less* = without	color	without color
❷ joyless			
❸ homeless			
❹ sleepless			
❺ wireless			
❻ seedless			

Name: _____   Date: _____

Combine and Create:
Suffix -*less*

Directions: Work with a partner to solve the riddles. Use the Word Bank for help.

Word Bank					
joyless	colorless	seedless	powerless	wireless	homeless

❶ I am a feeling that happens when you are very sad.

You would feel like me if you dropped your ice cream cone and got a bad grade on a vocabulary test all on the same day.

My base is only three letters long.

What am I? _____

❷ I describe black-and-white TVs.

I describe pictures in the newspaper.

I describe old photographs.

I have three syllables.

What am I? _____

❸ I describe how you might feel if you were not allowed to make choices.

I describe how the slaves might have felt before they met Harriet Tubman.

I describe how women felt before Susan B. Anthony worked to give them the right to vote.

What am I? _____

❹ I am a kind of grape.

Watermelons would be easier to eat if they were like me.

You use my base word to make your garden grow.

I have two syllables.

What am I? _____

❺ I describe cordless phones.

I describe laptop computers.

I don't trip you up!

You use my base to plug in your PlayStation®.

What am I? _____

❻ I describe people who do not have a place to live.

There is no place like my base.

What am I? _____

Name: _____   Date: _____

Read and Reason:
Suffix -less

Directions: Read the passage. Circle the words with the suffix -less. Then, answer the question.

Passage A

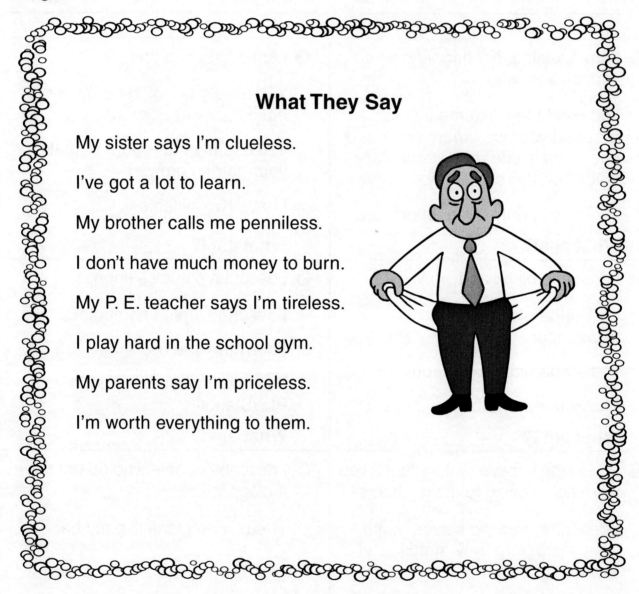

What They Say

My sister says I'm clueless.

I've got a lot to learn.

My brother calls me penniless.

I don't have much money to burn.

My P. E. teacher says I'm tireless.

I play hard in the school gym.

My parents say I'm priceless.

I'm worth everything to them.

Can you name someone or something in your own
life that is tireless or priceless?

Name: _____   Date: _____

Read and Reason:
Suffix -*less* (cont.)

Directions: Read the passage. Circle the words with the suffix -*less*. Then, answer the question.

Passage B

Edison's Bright Idea!

Thomas Edison dreamed of lighting the darkness. To do this, he invented an electric lightbulb. Before this, only flames from candles or gaslights could light the night. Most people were clueless about electricity. But Edison had ideas. He was also relentless in reaching his goal. One test led to another. Edison was tireless. He once said, "Genius is 1 percent inspiration and 99 percent perspiration." Finally, after countless attempts, he succeeded. He ran electricity through a bamboo thread inside an airless glass bulb. This was the first electric lightbulb to use at home. People everywhere were breathless when they learned of this discovery. It changed the world! Edison invented many things in his life. The electric lightbulb may have been his greatest discovery.

What does it mean when people were "breathless" when they learned that Edison had invented the light bulb?

Suffix *-ful*

Standards: Uses a variety of sentence structures to expand and embed ideas (McREL 2.3)
Uses conventions of spelling in written compositions (McREL 3.7)
Uses phonetic and structural analysis techniques, syntactic structure, and semantic context to decode unknown words (McREL 5.4)

Materials

- *Divide and Conquer: Suffix -ful* (page 142)

- *Combine and Create: Suffix -ful* (page 143)

- *Read and Reason: Suffix -ful* (pages 144–145)

Teaching Tips

- The suffix *-ful* means "full of." A suffix is a word part that comes at the end of a word and changes its meaning. For example, a *colorful* drawing is "full of" many colors. Likewise, a *playful* puppy is lively and "full of" energy to play.

- The suffix *-ful* attaches to bases that are whole words, such as *powerful* and *careful*. When explaining the meaning of a word with a suffix, the meaning of the suffix should always come first in the definition, even though the suffix is at the end of the word. For example, *joyful* means "full of joy," not "joy full of." As students offer definitions for words with suffixes, you may need to emphasize that their definitions must always make sense.

- When *-ful* is added to the end of a word, the spelling of that word does not change (e.g., *hope, hopeful*). Whenever a suffix is added to a base word that has more than one syllable and ends in "y," the "y" changes to "i." For example, when *-ful* is added to the word *beauty*, the "y" becomes an "i," making *beautiful*.

Guided Practice · · · · · · · · · · · ·

Activate Background Knowledge

1. Ask students to recall the meaning of the suffix *-less*. If you taught Lesson 18: Suffix *-less*, review how the suffix *-less* changes the meaning of a word to mean "without." Review the word *colorless* and write it on the board. Ask students to give examples of things that are colorless (black-and-white movies, newspapers, etc.). Then, ask students if a rainbow could be described as colorless. Lead a brief discussion about why the word *colorless* is not used to describe a rainbow. If necessary, explain that rainbows are not "without" color; they are "full of" color. Erase the suffix *-less* from the base *color* and add the suffix *-ful*. Explain that rainbows are color*ful*; they are literally "full of" colors.

2. Ask students to brainstorm additional words that may be used to describe rainbows. If they do not suggest the word *beautiful*, add it to the list. Write *colorful* and *beautiful* on the board (along with any other words with the *-ful* suffix that students mention). Ask them what the words *colorful* and *beautiful* have in common. Accept responses that refer to the *-ful* suffix and the idea of "full of."

Suffix -*ful* (cont.)

3. Tell students that -*ful* is a suffix meaning "full of." Put a slash between the -*ful* suffix and the base words in both *colorful* and *beautiful*. Next, ask students to generate other -*ful* words they may know. If they need assistance, use the following sentences as prompts:

   - When I got an A+ on my vocabulary test, I was full of joy. I felt _____. (*joyful*)

   - I have to take care around the stove so that I don't burn myself. I have to be _____. (*careful*)

   - Don't throw soda cans in the trashcan. It is a _____ thing to do. (*wasteful*)

Divide and Conquer

4. Before students begin this activity, tell them the following spelling tip. Whenever a suffix is added to a base word that has more than one syllable and ends in "y," the "y" changes to "i."

5. Distribute the *Divide and Conquer: Suffix -ful* activity sheet (page 142) to students. Students will Divide and Conquer words that contain intact bases. Guide students through the activity sheet, discussing how each word represents the idea of "full of." Then, have students think of examples that the words describe.

Combine and Create

6. Distribute the *Combine and Create: Suffix -ful* activity sheet (page 143) to students. Students will complete cloze sentences in friendly letters.

Read and Reason

7. Distribute the *Read and Reason: Suffix -ful* activity sheets (pages 144–145) to students. Have students read one or both passages and answer the comprehension questions on a separate sheet of paper. Ask them to circle the -*ful* words in the passage. If the passages are too difficult for independent

reading, ask students to read in pairs or follow along as you read aloud. Tell them to raise their hands when they hear a word with the -*ful* suffix. After you have finished reading, discuss the passage. Return to each of the -*ful* words and ask student volunteers to explain its meaning.

Extend and Explore

Choose from among the activities located in Appendix B to give students extra practice with the suffix -*ful*.

Answer Key

Divide and Conquer: Suffix -*ful* (page 142)

Students' answers for the "definition" section may vary; accept a range of answers.

1. colorful: full of; color; full of color
2. joyful: full of; joy; full of joy
3. playful: full of; play; full of play
4. hateful: full of; hate; full of hate
5. powerful: full of; power; full of power
6. beautiful: full of; beauty; full of beauty

Combine and Create: Suffix -*ful* (page 143)

1. joyful, playful
2. colorful, beautiful
3. powerful
4. hateful

Read and Reason: Suffix -*ful* (pages 144–145)

Passage A: *grateful, thankful, mouthful, earful, dreadful, skillfully, wonderful*

Students' answers will vary.

Passage B: *youthful, careful, harmful, painful, carefully, respectful, beautiful*

Students' answers will vary.

Name: _____   Date: _____

Divide and Conquer:
Suffix -*ful*

Directions: Break apart each word. Write the suffix and its meaning, the base word, and a simple definition for each word. An example has been done for you.

word	suffix means	base word	definition
1 colorful	-*ful* = full of	color	full of color
2 joyful			
3 playful			
4 hateful			
5 powerful			
6 beautiful			

Name: _____   Date: _____

Combine and Create:
Suffix *-ful*

Directions: Help these friends complete their letters. Use the Word Bank for help.

Word Bank					
playful	colorful	powerful	beautiful	hateful	joyful

❶ Dear Melissa,

I got a new puppy for my birthday!
I jumped for joy when I opened
the box and saw him. I felt so
_____!

My new puppy likes to play
fetch with the ball. He is very
_____.

Your friend,
Nathan

❷ Dear Deirdra,

Did you see the rainbow with all the
colors after the rain yesterday? It was
so _____! It
was so full of beauty! I think it was the
most _____
rainbow I've ever seen!

Your friend,
Jaico

❸ Dear Colin,

I think Abraham Lincoln is very
interesting. He ended slavery!
He kept our country together
during the Civil War. He must
have had a lot of power to be able
to do that. Lincoln was a very
_____ man.

Your friend,
Tyler

❹ Dear Arianna,

I don't like it when people say mean
things to each other. It is an unkind
and _____
thing to do. I am glad you are such a
kind friend!

Your friend,
Phoebe

Name: _____ Date: _____

Read and Reason:
Suffix *-ful*

Directions: Read the passage. Circle the words with the suffix *-ful*. Then, answer the question.

Passage A

Thanksgiving

Thanksgiving is always an interesting holiday at my home. Yet sometimes I wonder what I should be grateful for. Should I be thankful for the mouthful of turkey and the other good food I eat at Thanksgiving? Perhaps I should be thankful for a sister who gives me an earful whenever I borrow something of hers. Or maybe I should give thanks to my big brother who makes those dreadful noises after he eats. I know I should be grateful for my mom and dad who so skillfully prepare our Thanksgiving feast. Now I know. I need to be thankful for my wonderful family. I love them, and they love me.

What does the author mean when she says that her sister gives her an "earful"?

Name: _____   Date: _____

Read and Reason:
Suffix *-ful* (cont.)

Directions: Read the passage. Circle the words with the suffix *-ful*. Then, answer the question.

Passage B

Take Care of Your Skin

Want to keep your skin looking healthy and youthful? There are a few simple things you can do to protect this vital organ. First, be careful when you are in the sun. Sun rays can be harmful to your skin. Be sure to put sunscreen on exposed skin when you are outdoors. Also, wear a wide-brimmed hat to protect the skin on your face. Second, stay hydrated. Drink plenty of water. Skin that is well hydrated is less prone to chapping or flaking. Third, pay attention to cuts, odd freckles, moles, or growths on your skin. Untreated cuts can lead to painful and dangerous infections. Odd-looking moles and freckles can be a sign of a more serious skin problem. A doctor should carefully examine these. By being respectful of your skin, you can have healthy and beautiful skin that will last a lifetime.

What does "being respectful of your skin" mean?

Suffix -er

Standards: Uses a variety of sentence structures to expand and embed ideas (McREL 2.3)
Uses conventions of spelling in written compositions (McREL 3.7)
Uses phonetic and structural analysis techniques, syntactic structure, and semantic context to decode unknown words (McREL 5.4)

Materials

- Two pieces of string (one longer than the other)
- *Divide and Conquer: Suffix -er* (page 149)
- *Combine and Create: Suffix -er* (page 150)
- *Read and Reason: Suffix -er* (pages 151–152)

Teaching Tips

- The suffix *-er* means "more."
- A *suffix* is a word part that comes at the end of a word and changes its meaning. For example, because December is a winter month, it is colder—or "more" "cold"—than the summer month of June.
- When *-er* is added to an adjective, it compares two things: A hare is *quicker* than a tortoise.
- The bases in this lesson are whole-word adjectives that are familiar to most students.
- Before students Divide and Conquer, they learn that in three situations, adding the suffix *-er* to a word changes its spelling: (1) When a suffix is added to a word that has more than one syllable and ends in "y," the "y" changes to "i" (e.g., *angry* becomes *angrier*; *hungry* becomes *hungrier*); (2) When a word ends in "e," the "e" of the *-er* suffix is shared (e.g., *wise* becomes *wiser*); (3) When a word has one syllable and ends in a consonant, the final consonant is doubled before the *-er* suffix is attached (e.g., *big* becomes *bigger*).

Guided Practice · · · · · · · · · · · ·

Activate Background Knowledge

1. Draw two squares on the board, making one larger than the other. Ask students how the two squares are different. Accept their responses, drawing attention to responses that identify one box as larger or smaller than the other. Write *larger* and *smaller* on the board under the corresponding squares.

2. Next, show students two pieces of string, one of which is longer than the other. Ask students how the two pieces of string are different. Accept their responses, drawing attention to responses that identify one piece as longer or shorter than the other. Write *longer* and *shorter* on the board.

3. Ask students what the words *larger, smaller, longer,* and *shorter* have in common. Call attention to responses that identify the *-er* suffix and the idea of comparison or "more" than. Explain that *-er* is a suffix that means "more." Put a slash between the *-er* suffix and the base word in *larger, smaller, longer,* and *shorter*.

4. Next, ask students to generate other *-er* words that deal with the idea of "more." If students need assistance, use the following sentences as prompts:

    - Peppers are spicy, but jalapeños are _____. (*spicier*)
    - A kitten is _____ than a cat. (*smaller*)
    - A prairie is _____ than a valley. (*wider*)

Suffix -er (cont.)

Divide and Conquer

5. Distribute the *Divide and Conquer: Suffix -er* activity sheet (page 149) to students. Students will work with words that have intact bases. As they Divide and Conquer, encourage students to explain how the words represent the idea of "more." Because the *-er* suffix is used to compare two or more things, have students use the words in comparative sentences. For example, "A shout is *louder* than a whisper." This will help them learn how to use the *-er* suffix within the context of comparing two or more things.

6. Before beginning this Divide and Conquer, review the following spelling tips with students:

   - When *-er* is added to a word that has more than one syllable and ends in "y," the "y" changes to "i" (e.g., *happy* becomes *happier*).

   - When *-er* is added to a word ending in "e," the "e" of the suffix is shared (e.g., *nice* becomes *nicer*).

   - When *-er* is added to a word that ends in a consonant and has only one syllable, the last consonant is doubled (e.g., *big* becomes *bigger*).

Combine and Create

7. Distribute the *Combine and Create: Suffix -er* activity sheet (page 150) to students. Students will complete cloze sentences with the correct *-er* word. As students complete the activity, allow time for them to share their responses. Then, have students draw pictures that illustrate sentences that contain *-er* words.

Read and Reason

8. Distribute the *Read and Reason: Suffix -er* activity sheets (pages 151–152) to students. Have students read one or both passages and answer the comprehension questions on a separate sheet of paper. If the passages are too difficult for independent reading, ask students to read in pairs or follow along as you read aloud. If students read, ask them to circle the *-er* words. If you read, tell them to raise their hands when they hear a word with the *-er* suffix. List the words they identify. After you have finished reading, discuss the passage. You can also take this as an opportunity to discuss why *-er* attaches to base words when we compare objects as opposed to including the word *more* (e.g., *faster* vs. *more fast*). Return to the *-er* words and ask student volunteers to explain their meaning.

Extend and Explore

Choose from among the activities located in Appendix B to give students extra practice with the suffix *-er*.

Suffix -er *(cont.)*

Answer Key

Divide and Conquer: Suffix -er (page 149)

Students' answers for the "definition" section
may vary; accept a range of answers.

1. louder: more; loud; more loud
2. juicier: more; juicy; more juicy
3. lazier: more; lazy; more lazy
4. thinner: more; thin; more thin
5. smaller: more; small; more small
6. sadder: more; sad; more sad

Combine and Create: Suffix -er (page 150)

Part 1:

1. louder
2. hotter
3. lazier
4. noisier
5. thinner

Part 2: Students' drawings will vary.

Read and Reason: Suffix -er
(pages 151–152)

Passage A: *Faster, Smarter, Higher, humbler*

Students' answers will vary.

Passage B: *Faster, Higher, Stronger, faster,
higher, greater, ever-grander, swifter, safer,
costlier*

Students' answers will vary.

Name: _____ Date: _____

Divide and Conquer:
Suffix -er

Directions: Break apart each word. Write the suffix and its meaning, the base word, and a simple definition for each word. An example has been done for you.

word	suffix means	base word	definition
❶ louder	*-er* = more	loud	more loud
❷ juicier			
❸ lazier			
❹ thinner			
❺ smaller			
❻ sadder			

Name: _____   Date: _____

Combine and Create:
Suffix -er

Directions: Complete the sentences with the -er word that fits. Use the Word Bank to help you.

Word Bank				
hotter	noisier	lazier	louder	thinner

❶ When he was watching TV, Tyler couldn't hear the program, so he made the volume _____.

❷ Rainforests are _____ than wetlands because rainforests are closer to the equator.

❸ On Sunday, Devendra got up early, cooked breakfast, and did her homework, but Dana stayed in bed. Dana was _____ than Devendra.

❹ Dogs bark and make a lot of noise, but cats are quiet. Dogs are _____ than cats.

❺ Phoebe's dog used to be very fat because she never took it for walks. Now Phoebe walks her dog every day and her dog is _____.

Directions: Draw a picture to show what is happening in each sentence.

❶ The girl ran faster than the boy, so she beat him in the race.	**❷** I jumped in the rain puddles, but my brother did not. I was wetter than my brother.
❸ The airplane flew higher in the sky than the helicopter.	**❹** The trees in the park are taller than the bushes.

Name: _____ Date: _____

Read and Reason:
Suffix -er

Directions: Read the passage. Circle the words with the suffix -er. Then, answer the questions.

Passage A

A Conversation

Child: Hey, Mom. Did you know that I can run more fast than all the boys in my class?

Mother: Faster.

Child: And Mom, I think I am more smart than everyone in my class except Kim.

Mother: Smarter.

Child: Oh, and Mom, I can jump more high than all the kids in fourth grade.

Mother: Higher. And now my dear child, I'll bet that you want to tell me that you are also humbler than anyone in your class.

Child: More humble.

Would you like to have this child as a friend? Why or why not?

Name: _____ Date: _____

Read and Reason:
Suffix -er (cont.)

Directions: Read the passage. Circle the words with the suffix -er. Then, answer the question.

Passage B

Olympic Competitions

Every four years, the Summer Olympic Games take place. They are held in different cities around the world. During the Olympics, athletes compete in a variety of sports. The motto of the Olympics is "Faster, Higher, Stronger." Athletes try to run faster. They try to jump higher. And they try to show greater strength than ever before.

But it is not just the athletes who compete. The cities that host the Olympics also compete. Olympic cities create ever-grander displays to focus on themselves. Beijing, China, hosted the 2008 Summer Olympics. Beijing National Stadium is unique. It was meant to be greater than any Olympic stadium in the past. It has an unusual shape. This is why it is called the Bird's Nest.

The 2012 Summer Olympic Games were in London. They featured the Olympic Javelin Train. This was the name of a high-speed train that took visitors between Olympic sites. London residents hoped that the Javelin Train would provide Olympic visitors with swifter and safer travel than ever before.

Many of these projects turn out to be costlier than first thought. As a result, many cities lose money because of their need to compete. And in one way, at least, they lose.

Why do you think Olympic cities feel the need to compete with other Olympic cities?

Suffix -*est*

> **Standards:** Uses a variety of sentence structures to expand and embed ideas (McREL 2.3)
> Uses conventions of spelling in written compositions (McREL 3.7)
> Uses phonetic and structural analysis techniques, syntactic structure, and semantic context to decode unknown words (McREL 5.4)

Materials

- Three pieces of string (three different lengths)
- *Divide and Conquer: Suffix -est* (page 155)
- *Combine and Create: Suffix -est* (page 156)
- *Read and Reason: Suffix -est* (pages 157–158)

Teaching Tips

- The suffix -*est* means "most."
- A *suffix* is a word part that comes at the end of a word and changes its meaning. When -*est* is added to an adjective, it compares three or more things: *big, bigger, biggest.*
- Before students Divide and Conquer, they will learn that in three situations, adding the suffix -*est* to a word changes its spelling: (1) When a suffix is added to a word that ends in "y," the "y" changes to "i" (e.g., *angry* becomes *angriest*); (2) When a word ends in "e," the "e" of the -*est* suffix is shared (e.g., *wise* becomes *wisest*); (3) When a word has one syllable and ends in a consonant, the final consonant is doubled before the -*est* suffix is attached (e.g., *hot* becomes *hottest*).

Guided Practice · · · · · · · · · · · ·

Activate Background Knowledge

1. Draw three squares on the board, making each one larger than the last. Invite a student volunteer to come to the board and label each square according to its size by using the words *large, larger,* and *largest.* After the student labels each square, ask the class why he or she put the word *largest* under the largest square. Accept students' responses, drawing attention to those that identify the last square as the "most" large.

2. Show students three pieces of string, each of different lengths. Ask students how the three pieces of string are different. Next, ask them which string is shortest. Write the words *longest* and *shortest* on the board. Ask students what the words *longest* and *shortest* have in common. Accept students' responses, drawing attention to those that identify the -*est* suffix with the idea of comparison or "most."

3. Explain that -*est* is a suffix that means "most." Put a slash between the -*est* suffix and the base word in *longest* and *shortest.* Explain that the suffix -*est* is used to compare three or more things. Next, ask students to generate other -*est* words they may know. If students need assistance, use the following sentences as prompts:

   - My sister is four years old, and my brother is six years old. I am eight years old. I am the _____ of my siblings. (*oldest*)

   - At the dog park, my dog makes the most noise. He barks the _____ of all the dogs. (*loudest*)

   - Venus is hotter than all the other planets. It is the _____ planet. (*hottest*)

Suffix -est (cont.)

Divide and Conquer

4. Distribute the *Divide and Conquer: Suffix -est* activity sheet (page 155) to students. Students will work with words that have intact, familiar bases. As they Divide and Conquer, encourage students to explain how the words represent the idea of "most." Because the *-est* suffix is used to compare three or more things, have students use the words in comparative sentences (e.g., A shark is the *fiercest* predator, or February is the *shortest* month). This will help them learn how to use the suffix *-est* within the context of comparing objects.

5. Before beginning this Divide and Conquer, review the following spelling tips with students:

   • When *-est* is added to a word that has more than one syllable and ends in "y," the "y" changes to "i" (e.g., *happy* becomes *happiest*).

   • When *-est* is added to a word ending in "e," the "e" of the suffix is shared (e.g., *nice* becomes *nicest*).

   • When *-est* is added to a word that ends in a consonant and has only one syllable, the last consonant is doubled (e.g., *big* becomes *biggest*).

Combine and Create

6. Distribute the *Combine and Create: Suffix -est* activity sheet (page 156) to students. Students will complete cloze sentences in the form of friendly letters.

Read and Reason

7. Distribute the *Read and Reason: Suffix -est* activity sheets (pages 157–158) to students. Have students read one or both passages and answer the comprehension questions on a separate sheet of paper. If the passages are too difficult for independent reading, ask students to read in pairs or follow along as you read aloud. If they read, ask them to circle or list the *-est* words they find. If you

read, tell them to raise their hands when they hear a word with the *-est* suffix. List these for students. After you have finished reading, discuss the passage. Return to the *-est* words and ask student volunteers to explain their meaning.

Extend and Explore

Choose from among the activities located in Appendix B to give students extra practice with the suffix *-est*.

Answer Key

Divide and Conquer: Suffix -est (page 155)

Students' answers for the "definition" section may vary; accept a range of answers.

1. shortest: most; short; most short
2. fastest: most; fast; most fast
3. slowest: most; slow; most slow
4. smartest: most; smart; most smart
5. tallest: most; tall; most tall
6. richest: most; rich; most rich

Combine and Create: Suffix -est (page 156)

1. fastest, happiest, prettiest
2. tallest, smartest, bravest
3. cutest, slowest
4. richest, saddest

Read and Reason: Suffix -est (pages 157–158)

Passage A: *fastest, highest, farthest, longest, loudest*

Students' answers will vary.

Passage B: *biggest, tiniest, largest, greatest, smallest*

Students' answers will vary.

Name: _____ Date: _____

Divide and Conquer:
Suffix *-est*

Directions: Break apart each word. Write the suffix and its meaning, the base word, and a simple definition for each word. An example has been done for you.

word	suffix means	base word	definition
❶ shortest	*-est* = most	short	most short
❷ fastest			
❸ slowest			
❹ smartest			
❺ tallest			
❻ richest			

Name: _____ Date: _____

Combine and Create:
Suffix -est

Directions: Help these friends complete their letters by filling in the -est words. Use the Word Bank to help you.

Word Bank				
prettiest	cutest	slowest	fastest	happiest
richest	saddest	bravest	tallest	smartest

❶ Dear Roozah,

On Sunday, I ran in a race. I ran the _____ and won the race! When I finished, I jumped up and down and cheered. I felt like the _____ person in the world! My mom and dad gave me flowers. They were yellow, red, and pink. I put them in a vase. When I look at them, I think they are the _____ flowers in the world.

Your friend,
Zaniya

❷ Dear Colin,

I like to study the presidents. Abraham Lincoln was almost seven feet tall. He was our _____ president. He led our country through the Civil War and helped our country solve many problems. He was one of the _____ men in the country. He freed the slaves. That took a lot of courage. I think Lincoln was our _____ president.

Your friend,
Matthew

❸ Dear Arianna,

My favorite fairy tale is *Snow White and the Seven Dwarves*. The dwarves are so short and cute! They are the _____ characters! Their legs are so short it would take them a long time to run a race. They would be the _____ runners. But I would cheer for them the whole way!

Your friend,
Michelle

❹ Dear Jaico,

Last night, I read an article about a woman who had more than one million dollars! She lived in a mansion and had five cars! She was one of the _____ women in the world. But then she dropped her wallet and lost all that money! I bet she turned into one of the _____ people in the world!

Your friend,
Jeremy

Name: _____ Date: _____

Read and Reason:
Suffix -est

Directions: Read the passage. Circle the words with the suffix -est. Then, answer the question.

Passage A

Good, Better, Best

Good, better, best,

I'm better than all the rest.

I run the fastest, jump the highest,

Get perfect scores on tests,

Swim the farthest, sleep the longest,

Laugh loudest when we jest.

Good, better, best,

I'm better than all the rest.

I'm so good at bragging, too,

You may think I'm just a pest.

Why do you think the writer of this poem might be a pest?

Name: _____   Date: _____

Read and Reason:
Suffix -est (cont.)

Directions: Read the passage. Circle the words with the suffix -est. Then, answer the question.

Passage B

Our World—Big and Small!

Which country in the world is the biggest? It all depends. In terms of the most land, Russia is the biggest. Russia has over 6 million square miles of land. The United States comes in third place in terms of land area with a little over 3 million square miles. Vatican City, however, which is located in Rome, is the tiniest country in terms of land. This tiny country is made up of less than 1 square mile of land.

However, in population, China is the largest. Over 1.3 billion people live in China. India is not far behind China. Over 1.2 billion people call India home. Perhaps, someday India can claim to have the greatest population in the world. Today, more than 1 of every 3 people in the world lives in one of these two countries. Again, the United States comes in third place in terms of population. Just over 300 million people reside in the United States. The Pitcairn Islands has the smallest population of any country in the world. Fewer than 100 people live on these islands. The world is indeed made up of countries of all shapes and sizes.

Would you rather live in a country with a large or small population?
Explain why you think this.

Suffix *-ly*

Standards: Uses a variety of sentence structures to expand and embed ideas (McREL 2.3)
Uses conventions of spelling in written compositions (McREL 3.7)
Uses phonetic and structural analysis techniques, syntactic structure, and semantic context to decode unknown words (McREL 5.4)

Materials

- *Divide and Conquer: Suffix -ly* (page 162)

- *Combine and Create: Suffix -ly* (page 163)

- *Read and Reason: Suffix -ly* (pages 164–165)

Teaching Tips

- The suffix *-ly* means "in a _____ way."

- A *suffix* is a word part that comes at the end of a word and changes its meaning (e.g., turtles move *slowly*, or "in a slow way," while rabbits move *quickly*, or "in a quick way").

- Before students Divide and Conquer, they will learn that in two situations, adding the suffix *-ly* to a word changes its spelling: (1) When the suffix *-ly* is added to a word with more than one syllable that ends in "y," the "y" changes to "i" (e.g., *happy* becomes *happily*); (2) When the suffix *-ly* is added to a word ending in "le," the final "e" is dropped (e.g., *gentle* becomes *gently*).

Guided Practice · · · · · · · · · · · ·

Activate Background Knowledge

1. Begin by asking students to turn and talk with partners in their "indoor" or "whisper" voices. Ask students to describe how they talked. In what way did they use their voices? Accept responses, calling attention to those that refer to talking *softly* or *quietly*.

2. Write the words *softly* and *quietly* on the board. Next, ask students to talk to each other in "playground" or "outside" voices. Ask them to describe how they spoke to each other. Accept responses, calling attention to those that refer to talking *loudly* or *noisily*.

3. Write the words *loudly* and *noisily* on the board. Ask students what the words *softly, quietly, loudly,* and *noisily* have in common. Accept students' responses, calling attention to those that identify the *-ly* suffix and the idea of doing something "in a particular way."

4. Tell students that *-ly* is a suffix that means "in a _____ way." For example, speaking *softly* means "to speak in a soft way"; speaking *loudly* means "to speak in a loud way."

5. Ask students to generate other words with the *-ly* suffix that they may know. If students need help, use the following sentences as prompts:

   - When the toddler dropped his ice cream cone on the ground, he cried _____. (*sadly*)

Suffix -ly (cont.)

- When I got a new puppy for my birthday, I jumped up and down _____. (*happily*)

- The turtle crawled along the sand _____. (*slowly*)

Divide and Conquer

6. Before beginning this Divide and Conquer, review the following spelling tips with students:

   - When *-ly* is added to a word that has more than one syllable and ends in "y," the "y" changes to "i" (e.g., *happy* becomes *happily*).

   - When *-ly* is added to a word ending in *-le*, the final "e" is dropped (e.g., *gentle* becomes *gently*).

7. Distribute the *Divide and Conquer: Suffix -ly* activity sheet (page 162) to students. Students will work with words that have intact, familiar bases. As students Divide and Conquer, encourage them to explain how the words represent the idea of doing an action in a particular way. As students work with the *-ly* words, ask them to give examples of actions that the words can be used to describe (e.g., What is something you may do *sadly*?). Pairing the words with the actions they may describe will help students learn the meaning of the *-ly* suffix.

Combine and Create

8. Distribute the *Combine and Create: Suffix -ly* activity sheet (page 163) to students. Students rewrite sentences using words with the *-ly* suffix. After students complete their sentences, allow time for them to share. Talking about new words with peers is an effective strategy for helping students learn new vocabulary.

Read and Reason

9. Distribute the *Read and Reason: Suffix -ly* activity sheet (pages 164–165) to students. Have students read one or both passages and answer the comprehension questions on a separate sheet of paper. If the passages are too difficult for independent reading, ask students to read in pairs or follow along as you read aloud. If they read, ask them to circle the *-ly* words they encounter. If you read, tell them to raise their hands when they hear a word with the *-ly* suffix. After you have finished reading, discuss the passage. Return to each of the *-ly* words and ask student volunteers to explain their meaning.

Extend and Explore

Choose from among the activities located in Appendix B to give students extra practice with the suffix *-ly*.

Suffix *-ly* (cont.)

Answer Key

Divide and Conquer: Suffix *-ly* (page 162)

Students' answers for the "definition" section may vary; accept a range of answers.

1. wisely: in a _____ way; wise; in a wise way
2. sadly: in a _____ way; sad; in a sad way
3. happily: in a _____ way; happy; in a happy way
4. slowly: in a _____ way; slow; in a slow way
5. quickly: in a _____ way; quick; in a quick way
6. lazily: in a _____ way; lazy; in a lazy way

Combine and Create: Suffix *-ly* (page 163)

1. quickly; Jairo ran the race quickly. OR Jairo quickly ran the race.
2. carefully; Omar carried the hot soup carefully. OR Omar carefully carried the hot soup.
3. lazily; The cat rested on the couch lazily. OR The cat lazily rested on the couch.
4. quietly; During silent reading, we read quietly. OR During silent reading, we quietly read.

Read and Reason: Suffix *-ly* (pages 164–165)

Passage A: *inquisitively, excitedly, gingerly, anxiously, quickly, briskly*

Students' answers will vary.

Passage B: *carefully, highly, Finally, quickly, orally, silently, definitely*

Students' answers will vary.

Word Sort (page 166)

2 syllables: *biggest, careless, gently, hateful, hopeless, hottest, joyless, loudest, loudly, oldest, painful, sadly, slowly, smaller, thinner, wireless, wiser, youthful*

3 syllables: *angrier, beautiful, colorful, happily, juicier, prettiest, sugarless*

Could describe the way an action is done: *gently, happily, loudly, sadly, slowly*

Could not describe the way an action is done: *angrier, beautiful, biggest, careless, colorful, hateful, hopeless, hottest, joyless, juicier, loudest, oldest, painful, prettiest, smaller, sugarless, thinner, wireless, wiser, youthful*

Spelling change to add suffix: *angrier, beautiful, biggest, gently, happily, hottest, juicier, prettiest, thinner, wiser*

No spelling change to add suffix: *careless, colorful, hateful, hopeless, joyless, loudest, loudly, oldest, painful, sadly, slowly, smaller, sugarless, wireless, youthful*

Name: _____   Date: _____

Divide and Conquer:
Suffix -*ly*

Directions: Break apart each word. Write the suffix and its meaning, the base word, and a simple definition for each word. An example has been done for you.

word	suffix means	base word	definition
1 wisely	*-ly* = in a _____ way	wise	in a wise way
2 sadly			
3 happily			
4 slowly			
5 quickly			
6 lazily			

Name: _____ Date: _____

Combine and Create:
Suffix -*ly*

Directions: Read each sentence. Make a new word out of the words in bold using the -*ly* suffix. Then, use the new word in a sentence.

Example:

When my brother wrecked my bike, I jumped up and down **in an angry way**.

Word: <u>angrily</u>

Sentence: <u>When my brother wrecked my bike, I angrily jumped up and down.</u>

❶ Jairo ran the race **in a quick way**.

Word: _____

Sentence: _____

❷ Omar carried the hot soup **in a careful way**.

Word: _____

Sentence: _____

❸ The cat rested on the couch **in a lazy way**.

Word: _____

Sentence: _____

❹ During silent reading, we read **in a quiet way**.

Word: _____

Sentence: _____

Name: _____ Date: _____

Read and Reason:
Suffix *-ly*

Directions: Read the passage. Circle the words with the suffix *-ly*. Then, answer the question.

Passage A

Good Advice

"Where are you going, Tommy?" Mom asked inquisitively.

"Joe and I are going to the movies!" I answered excitedly.

"What movie are you going to see?" Dad asked as he gingerly rubbed his chin.

"*The Monster That Ate New York City*," I replied anxiously. "I think it's a scary one."

"Well just be sure to close your eyes quickly whenever the loud music comes on," chimed Mom as I briskly walked out the door.

Why do you think the young person going to the movies
anxiously replied to his father's question?

Name: _____   Date: _____

Read and Reason:
Suffix -*ly* (cont.)

Directions: Read the passage. Circle the words with the suffix -*ly*. Then, answer the question.

Passage B

How to Enjoy Reading

Although most people know how to read, not everyone likes to read. But reading can be a pleasurable experience.

First, you need to carefully choose a book or other material to read. A fabulous place to find good books is your public library. If you have difficulty finding a good book, ask a librarian. Librarians are highly trained to help people match books with their interests. They can even find a book for you that is audio-recorded. That way, you can listen to the words while reading them, too.

Once you have your book, find a comfortable place. This can be an easy chair at home or a lawn chair in your yard. Some people like to read in bed. Others like to read on a beach towel. Just be sure to find a place that is comfortable for you. Be sure that your reading place is well lit. You need your eyes to read and your eyes need light. But too much light can make reading difficult. Most people prefer a place to read that is not too noisy. Too much noise can distract you from what you are reading. Finally, many readers like having a glass of water close by. Snacks add to the reading experience, too.

Now you are ready to start reading. Try not to read too quickly. You should read at a pace that you find comfortable. Feel free to read orally or silently to yourself—it really doesn't matter. Reading should be a fun experience. These tips will definitely help make reading enjoyable!

What else could you do to make reading more enjoyable?

Name: _____   Date: _____

Review:
Word Sort

Directions: Write the words in the appropriate boxes. Be ready to explain your choices. Some words can go in more than one box.

Word Bank						
angrier	beautiful	biggest	careless	colorful	gently	happily
hateful	hopeless	hottest	joyless	juicier	loudest	loudly
oldest	painful	prettiest	sadly	slowly	smaller	sugarless
thinner	wireless	wiser	youthful			

2 Syllables	3 Syllables

Could Describe the Way An Action Is Done	Could Not Describe the Way An Action Is Done

Spelling Change to Add Suffix	No Spelling Change to Add Suffix

References Cited

Baumann, James F., Elizabeth Carr Edwards, George Font, Cathleen A. Tereshinski, Edward J. Kame'enui, and Stephen Olejnik. 2002. "Teaching Morphemic and Contextual Analysis to Fifth-Grade Students." *Reading Research Quarterly* 37: 150–176.

Baumann, James F., George Font, Elizabeth Carr Edwards, and Eileen Boland. 2005. "Strategies for Teaching Middle-Grade Students to Use Word-Part and Context Clues to Expand Reading Vocabulary." In *Teaching and Learning Vocabulary: Bringing Research to Practice*, edited by E. H. Hiebert and M. L. Kamil, 179–205. Mahwah, NJ: Erlbaum.

Bear, Donald R., Marcia R. Invernizzi, Shane Templeton, and Francine R. Johnston. 2011. *Words Their Way: Word Study for Phonics, Vocabulary, and Spelling Instruction.* 7th ed. Upper Saddle River, NJ: Prentice Hall.

Beck, Isabel L., Margaret G. McKeown, and Linda Kucan. 2002. *Bringing Words to Life: Robust Vocabulary Instruction.* New York: Guilford.

Beck, Isabel L., Margaret G. McKeown, Richard C. Omanson, and Charles A. Perfetti. 1982. "Effects of Long-Term Vocabulary Instruction on Lexical Access and Reading Comprehension." *Journal of Educational Psychology* 74: 506–521.

Biemiller, Andrew. 2005. "Size and Sequence in Vocabulary Development: Implications of Choosing Words for Primary Grade Vocabulary." In *Teaching and Learning Vocabulary: Bringing Research to Practice*, edited by E. H. Hiebert and M. L. Kamil, 223–242. Mahwah, NJ: Erlbaum.

Biemiller, Andrew, and Naomi Slonim. 2001. "Estimating Root Word Vocabulary Growth in Normative and Advantaged Populations: Evidence for a Common Sequence of Vocabulary Acquisition." *Journal of Educational Psychology* 93: 498–520.

Blachowicz, Camille, and Peter J. Fisher. 2009. *Teaching Vocabulary in All Classrooms.* 4th ed. Upper Saddle River, NJ: Pearson/Merrill/Prentice Hall.

Blachowicz, Camille, Peter J. Fisher, Donna Ogle, and Susan Watts-Taffe. 2006. "Vocabulary: Questions from the Classroom." *Reading Research Quarterly* 41 (4): 524–538.

Carlisle, Joanne F. 2000. "Awareness of the Structure and Meaning of Morphologically Complex Words: Impact on Reading." *Reading and Writing: An Interdisciplinary Journal* 12: 169–190.

———. 2010. "Effects of Instruction in Morphological Awareness on Literacy Achievement: An Integrative Review." *Reading Research Quarterly* (45): 464–487.

Cunningham, Patricia M. 2004. *Phonics They Use: Words for Reading and Writing.* New York: Longman.

Fuchs, Lynn S., and Douglas Fuchs. 1998. "Treatment Validity: A Unifying Concept for Reconceptualizing the Identification of Learning Disabilities." *Learning Disabilities Research and Practice* 13 (4): 204–219.

Graves, Michael F., and Susan Watts-Taffe. 2002. "The Place of Word Consciousness in a Research-Based Vocabulary Program." In *What Research Has to Say About Reading Instruction,* edited by A. E. Farstrup and S. J. Samuels, 140–165. Newark, DE: International Reading Association.

References Cited (cont.)

Griffiths, Amy-Jane, Lorien B. Parson, Matthew K. Burns, Amanda VanDerHeyden, and W. David Tilly. 2007. *Response to intervention: Policy considerations and implementation*. Alexandria, VA: National Association of Special Education, Inc.

Harmon, Janis M., Wanda B. Hedrick, and Karen D. Wood. 2005. "Research on Vocabulary Instruction in the Content Areas: Implications for Struggling Readers." *Reading & Writing Quarterly* (21): 261–280.

Kame'enui, Edward, Douglas W. Carnine, and Roger Freschi. 1982. "Effects of text construction and instructional procedures for teaching word meanings on comprehension and recall." *Reading Research Quarterly* 17: 367–388.

Kieffer, Michael J., and Nonie K. Lesaux. 2007. "Breaking Down Words to Build Meaning: Morphology, Vocabulary, and Reading Comprehension in the Urban Classroom." *The Reading Teacher* 61: 134–144.

Lehr, Fran, Jean Osborn, and Elfrieda H. Hiebert. 2011. "Research-Based Practices in Early Reading Series: A Focus on Vocabulary." Accessed January 7, 2013. http://prel.org/media/160751/vocabulary2011.pdf.

Mountain, Lee. 2005. "ROOTing out meaning: More morphemic analysis for primary pupils." *The Reading Teacher* 58: 742–749.

Nagy, William, Richard C. Anderson, Marlene Schommer, Judith Scott, and Anne Stallman. 1989. "Morphological Families in the Internal Lexicon." *Reading Research Quarterly* (24): 262–282.

Nagy, William, and Judith Scott. 2000. "Vocabulary Processes." In *Handbook of Reading Research, Volume III*, edited by Michael L. Kamil, Peter B. Mosenthal, P. David Pearson, and Rebecca Barr, 269–284. Mahwah, NJ: Erlbaum.

National Governors Association Center for Best Practices and Council of Chief State School Officers. 2011. *Common Core State Standards Initiative: The Standards*. Accessed October 10, 2012. http://www.corestandards.org/the-standards.

Porter-Collier, I. M. 2010. "Teaching vocabulary through the roots approach in order to increase comprehension and metacognition." Unpublished Master's degree project. Akron, OH: University of Akron.

Rasinski, Timothy, and Nancy Padak. 2008. *From Phonics to Fluency*, 2nd ed. New York: Longman.

Stahl, Steven A., and Marilyn M. Fairbanks. 1986. "The Effects of Vocabulary Instruction: A Model-Based Meta-Analysis." *Review of Educational Research* 56: 72–110.

Extend and Explore

The following activities can provide extra prefix or suffix practice or can be shared with parents as a form of differentiating instruction. In some cases, reproducibles of activity sheets are included in Appendix C and in the Digital Resources.

Authors and Illustrators

Select 5–10 words containing the targeted prefix or suffix and put them on the board. Students may work individually or with a partner to write a story that includes each of those words. Once they have finished their stories, students trade them with another student or partner team. Each team reads the new story and then draws a picture to illustrate some part of it. When they have finished, they share illustrations with the story's author(s), explaining what they drew and why.

Students will also enjoy reading their stories aloud. After everyone has read, point out the variety of ways in which the targeted words can be used. Invite students to talk about their stories or ask questions of each other. Talking about the words is a good way to give students practice using them.

Extend and Explore (cont.)

Concentration (or Memory)

Select 8–10 words containing a prefix or suffix. Make double sets of word cards for each (or put the word and its definition on separate cards). Shuffle the cards and put them all face down on a table. Players take turns trying to make matches. The player with the most cards wins the game.

Go Fish

Select 4–6 words containing a prefix. For each, add suffixes or additional prefixes to create a set of four words (e.g., *refund*, *refunded*, *refunding*, *refundable*). Use these to play *Go Fish*.

Extend and Explore *(cont.)*

List-Group-Label or Word Webs

Provide a prefix or suffix. Ask students to brainstorm words containing it. Write these on the board. Then, ask small groups to work with the words by:

- Listing related terms and providing labels for them

- Developing a graphic, such as a web, that shows how the words are related

Extend and Explore (cont.)

Odd Word Out

Ask students to compare and contrast related words by choosing a word that does not "fit" and then explaining why. This can be used as a small-group discussion activity; whole-group conversation should follow. The following is an example:

Look at the four words. Write the one that does not belong on the line. Then, write how the other words are the same.

precook

preheat

premixed

pretest

The word that does not belong is _____. The other words are the same because _____.

To develop this activity, select three or four words, two or three of which share some characteristic. Words could be related semantically or syntactically. Words could also be related by the presence or absence of word parts. The groups of words you select will often have multiple answers, which promotes students' thinking about the many ways in which words can be related to one another. (*Note:* When students become accustomed to this activity, they can select sets of words for their peers to consider.)

Extend and Explore *(cont.)*

Root Word Riddles

Who does not enjoy the brain-teasing process of solving a riddle? This strategy invites students to create and guess riddles with words from the same prefix or suffix.

Give students a list of words that contain the targeted prefix or suffix. Each pair's job is to devise riddles for other students to solve. (You may want to model riddle creation for students.) The following is an example for the word *invisible*:

1. I have four syllables.

2. I have two word parts.

3. One part means "not."

4. The other means "see."

5. I mean "not perceptible to the human eye."

   What am I?

Extend and Explore (cont.)

Scattergories®

Make a matrix (see scattergoriesmatrix.doc in the Digital Resources) with prefixes along one dimension and suffixes along the other. The following is an example:

Prefixes	-ing	-ed	-ion
re-			
in-, im-, il-			
un-			

Ask students to work with partners to generate as many words as possible for each cell of the matrix.

Extend and Explore (cont.)

Sketch to Stretch

Provide words with prefixes or suffixes written on slips of paper. Distribute these to students. Ask them to sketch something that reveals the word meaning. Then, ask them to share their sentences with other classmates to guess what they have drawn.

20 Questions

Have students take turns asking questions that will help them figure out a "mystery" word that contains the targeted prefix or suffix. (If you and your students keep a word wall of words containing the prefix or suffix, select words from it.) They can ask up to 20 *Yes* or *No* questions to try to determine the word.

Extend and Explore (cont.)

Wordo

This vocabulary game is a wonderful way for students to play with new words they are learning.

List 16 or 25 words containing the targeted prefix or suffix on the board. Duplicate a WORDO card (see wordomatrix.pdf in the Digital Resources) for each student. Ask each student to choose a free box and mark it. Then, have them write one of the words in each of the remaining boxes. Students choose whatever box they wish for each word.

Now call a clue for each word: the definition, a synonym, an antonym, or a sentence with the target word deleted. Students figure out the correct target word, and then put an X through it. (If you want to clear the sheets and play again, use small scraps of paper or other items to mark the squares.) When a student has Xs or markers in a row, a column, a diagonal, or four corners, he or she can call out, "WORDO."

Extend and Explore (cont.)

Word Puzzles

Either you or your students can make crossword puzzles or word searches using the website http://www.puzzlemaker.com.

Word Skits

List 8–10 words containing the targeted prefix or suffix on the board. Divide the class into teams of 3–4. Each team chooses one word and writes its definition on an index card. Working together, they create a skit or situation that shows the meaning of the word. The skit is performed without words. Classmates try to guess the word being shown. Once the word is correctly identified, the definition is read out loud.

Extend and Explore *(cont.)*

Word Pyramid

This activity asks students to choose one word with the targeted prefix or suffix and explore it from different perspectives by "building" a pyramid of synonyms and antonyms. Duplicate a Word Pyramid template (see wordpyramid.pdf in the Digital Resources) for each student or pair of students. Put the targeted prefix or suffix on the board. Ask students to identify one word containing the prefix or suffix and write it in the first blank at the top. Tell them they will complete the pyramid by filling in the blanks. The second line asks for two antonyms. The third line asks for three synonyms. The fourth line asks them to provide their own definition of the word, and the fifth line asks them to write a sentence using the targeted word.

Encourage students to share their word pyramids. When students have chosen the same word, point out the variety of ways in which it can be used. When students have worked on different words, ask why they chose their words. Talking about the words is a good way to give students practice using them.

Extend and Explore *(cont.)*

Word Sorts

Select about 20 words containing the targeted prefix or suffix. Put the words on index cards or slips of paper. (If you are introducing Word Sorts to students, you may also want to put the words on a blank transparency and cut them apart so that you can demonstrate the process of sorting the words.)

Provide one set of word cards to each pair of students. Ask students to group the words. Remind them that they will be asked to explain their groupings. Some criteria for grouping include:

- Presence/absence of a root (e.g., has a suffix/does not have a suffix)

- Number of syllables

- Presence/absence of a long vowel sound (in general, or a particular long vowel sound)

After a few minutes, invite students to tell about one of their groups, both the words contained in it and the reason for putting them together. If time permits, ask students to sort the same set of words repeatedly. Each sorting provides students with another opportunity to think about both the words and their component parts.

Extend and Explore *(cont.)*

Word Spokes

Duplicate a Word Spokes template (see wordspokes.pdf in the Digital Resources) for each student or pair of students. Put the targeted prefix or suffix on the board. Ask students to identify enough words containing the prefix or suffix to complete the organizer. You may want to ask students to add sentences or illustrations of selected words as well. Conclude the activity with sharing.

Word War

Provide words containing the targeted prefix or suffix written on cards. Play the card game War with them. Each player turns up a card. The person whose card 1) comes first in alphabetical order, 2) has more letters, or 3) has more syllables wins the round as long as he or she can say both words and their meanings. If the words are similar, players draw again, and the same rules apply. The player who wins this war takes all the cards. A player who gets all his or her partner's cards wins the game.

Extend and Explore (cont.)

Word Theater

Select and list at least 10 words that contain the targeted prefix or suffix and that can be dramatized easily. List the words so that everyone can see them. Ask students to find a partner, read the list of words to each other, and then choose a word. Tell them they have two minutes to decide how to get the word's meaning across by acting it out. Remind them that they cannot speak during the pantomime.

Ask each team to act out its word while other students try to guess the word. Make sure the list of words is visible so that students can keep reading and rereading the words as they try to figure out which one is being pantomimed. As students look for connections between the acting and the word list, they will better understand the concepts each word represents.

Scattergories Matrix

Directions: Work with a partner to create as many words using the table.

Prefixes			

Wordo Matrix

Directions: Listen to your teacher to know how to complete the matrix.

Wordo Matrix (cont.)

Word Pyramid

Directions: Complete the organizer.

_____ **word**

_____ _____ **antonyms**

_____ _____ _____ **synonyms**

_____

define the word

Write a sentence using the word.

_____

_____

_____

_____

_____

_____

Word Spokes

Directions: Complete the organizer. Then, answer the questions.

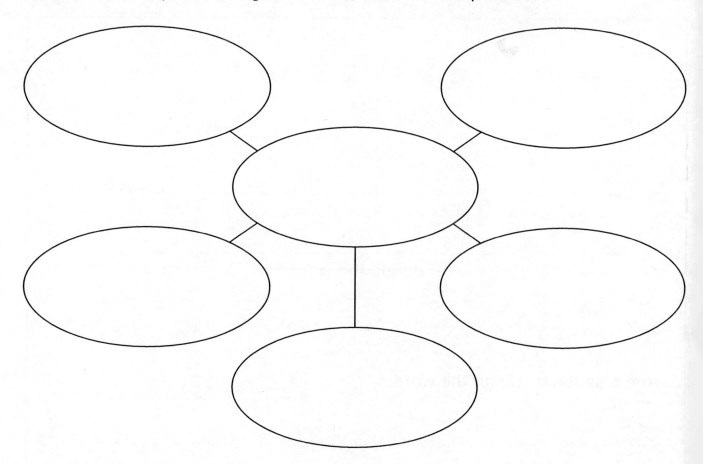

Choose a different word from your cluster for each of the following:

❶ Pick one of the words and write 2 **synonyms**.

Word _____ 1. _____ 2. _____

❷ Pick one of the words and write 2 **antonyms**.

Word _____ 1. _____ 2. _____

❸ Pick one of the words and write your own definition.

_____

❹ Pick one of the words and use it in a sentence.

_____

❺ Take the last word and do any one of the activities in 1–4.

Blank Flashcards

Blank Flashcards (cont.)

Digital Resources

Accessing the Digital Resources

The Digital Resources can be downloaded by following these steps:

1. Go to **www.tcmpub.com/digital**

2. Use the ISBN number to redeem the Digital Resources.

ISBN

ISBN-13: 978-1-4258-1103-7

90000

9 781425 811037

3. Respond to the question using the book.

4. Follow the prompts on the Content Cloud website to sign in or create a new account.

5. The redeemed content will now be on your My Content screen. Click on the product to look through the Digital Resources. All files can be downloaded, while some files can also be previewed, opened, and shared.

Page	Activity Sheet	Filename
26	Divide and Conquer: Two-Syllable Compound Words	dctwosyllable.pdf
27	Combine and Create: Two-Syllable Compound Words	cctwosyllable.pdf
28–29	Read and Reason: Two-Syllable Compound Words	rrtwosyllable.pdf
32	Divide and Conquer: Three-Syllable Compound Words	dcthreesyllable.pdf
33	Combine and Create: Three-Syllable Compound Words	ccthreesyllable.pdf
34–35	Read and Reason: Three-Syllable Compound Words	rrthreesyllable.pdf
38	Divide and Conquer: Negative Prefix *un-*	dcnegprefixun.pdf
39	Combine and Create: Negative Prefix *un-*	ccnegprefixun.pdf
40–41	Read and Reason: Negative Prefix *un-*	rrnegprefixun.pdf
44	Divide and Conquer: Negative Prefix *in-*	dcnegprefixin.pdf
45	Combine and Create: Negative Prefix *in-*	ccnegprefixin.pdf
46–47	Read and Reason: Negative Prefix *in-*	rrnegprefixin.pdf
50	Divide and Conquer: Negative Prefixes *im-* and *il-*	dcnegprefixesimil.pdf
51	Combine and Create: Negative Prefixes *im-* and *il-*	ccnegprefixesimil.pdf
52–53	Read and Reason: Negative Prefixes *im-* and *il-*	rrnegprefixesimil.pdf
56	Divide and Conquer: Negative Prefix *dis-*	dcnegprefixdis.pdf
57	Combine and Create: Negative Prefix *dis-*	ccnegprefixdis.pdf
58–59	Read and Reason: Negative Prefix *dis-*	rrnegprefixdis.pdf
60	Review: Magic Square	magicsquare.pdf
63	Divide and Conquer: Prefix *re-*	dcprefixre.pdf
64	Combine and Create: Prefix *re-*	ccprefixre.pdf

Digital Resources (cont.)

Page	Activity Sheet	Filename
65–66	Read and Reason: Prefix re-	rrprefixre.pdf
69	Divide and Conquer: Prefix pre-	dcprefixpre.pdf
70	Combine and Create: Prefix pre-	ccprefixpre.pdf
71–72	Read and Reason: Prefix pre-	rrprefixpre.pdf
75	Divide and Conquer: Prefix ex-	dcprefixex.pdf
76	Combine and Create: Prefix ex-	ccprefixex.pdf
77–78	Read and Reason: Prefix ex-	rrprefixex.pdf
81	Divide and Conquer: Prefix sub-	dcprefixsub.pdf
82	Combine and Create: Prefix sub-	ccprefixsub.pdf
83–84	Read and Reason: Prefix sub-	rrprefixsub.pdf
87	Divide and Conquer: Prefix de-	dcprefixde.pdf
88	Combine and Create: Prefix de-	ccprefixde.pdf
89–90	Read and Reason: Prefix de-	rrprefixde.pdf
94	Divide and Conquer: Prefixes co- and con-	dcprefixescocon.pdf
95	Combine and Create: Prefixes co- and con-	ccprefixescocon.pdf
96–97	Read and Reason: Prefixes co- and con-	rrprefixescocon.pdf
98–99	Review: Crossword Puzzle	crossword.pdf
103	Divide and Conquer: Prefixes uni- and unit-	dcprefixesuniunit.pdf
104	Combine and Create: Prefixes uni- and unit-	ccprefixesuniunit.pdf
105–106	Read and Reason: Prefixes uni- and unit-	rrprefixesuniunit.pdf
109	Divide and Conquer: Prefix bi-	dcprefixbi.pdf
110	Combine and Create: Prefix bi-	ccprefixbi.pdf
111–112	Read and Reason: Prefix bi-	rrprefixbi.pdf
115	Divide and Conquer: Prefix tri-	dcprefixtri.pdf
116	Combine and Create: Prefix tri-	ccprefixtri.pdf
117–118	Read and Reason: Prefix tri-	rrprefixtri.pdf
121	Divide and Conquer: Prefixes quart- and quadr-	dcprefixesquartquadr.pdf
122	Combine and Create: Prefixes quart- and quadr-	ccprefixesquartquadr.pdf
123–124	Read and Reason: Prefixes quart- and quadr-	rrprefixesquartquadr.pdf
128	Divide and Conquer: Prefix multi-	dcprefixmulti.pdf
129	Combine and Create: Prefix multi-	ccprefixmulti.pdf
130–131	Read and Reason: Prefix multi-	rrprefixmulti.pdf
132	Review: Scrambles	scrambles.pdf
136	Divide and Conquer: Suffix -less	dcsuffixless.pdf
137	Combine and Create: Suffix -less	ccsuffixless.pdf
138–139	Read and Reason: Suffix -less	rrsuffixless.pdf

Digital Resources *(cont.)*

Page	Activity Sheet	Filename
142	Divide and Conquer: Suffix *-ful*	dcsuffixful.pdf
143	Combine and Create: Suffix *-ful*	ccsuffixful.pdf
144–145	Read and Reason: Suffix *-ful*	rrsuffixful.pdf
149	Divide and Conquer: Suffix *-er*	dcsuffixer.pdf
150	Combine and Create: Suffix *-er*	ccsuffixer.pdf
151–152	Read and Reason: Suffix *-er*	rrsuffixer.pdf
155	Divide and Conquer: Suffix *-est*	dcsuffixest.pdf
156	Combine and Create: Suffix *-est*	ccsuffixest.pdf
157–158	Read and Reason: Suffix *-est*	rrsuffixest.pdf
162	Divide and Conquer: Suffix *-ly*	dcsuffixly.pdf
163	Combine and Create: Suffix *-ly*	ccsuffixly.pdf
164–165	Read and Reason: Suffix *-ly*	rrsuffixly.pdf
166	Review: Word Sort	wordsort.pdf
N/A	Correlation to Standards	mcrel.pdf ccss.pdf tesolwida.pdf
169–181	Extend and Explore	extendexplore.pdf
182	Scattergories Matrix	scattergoriesmatrix.doc
183–184	Wordo Matrix	wordomatrix.pdf
185	Word Pyramid	wordpyramid.pdf
186	Word Spokes	wordspokes.pdf
187–202	Prefixes Flashcards	prefixesflashcards.pdf
203–208	Suffixes Flashcards	suffixesflashcards.pdf
209–210	Blank Flashcards	blankflashcards.pdf

Notes

#51103—Starting with Prefixes and Suffixes

Notes

Notes